LIFE AND CAREER TRANSFORMATION

MASTERING YOUR MINDSET, HABITS, AND SKILLS FOR A FULFILLING LIFE

LAMMUANSANG TOMBING

Copyright © Lammuansang Tombing
All Rights Reserved.

This book has been self-published with all reasonable efforts taken to make the material error-free by the author. No part of this book shall be used, reproduced in any manner whatsoever without written permission from the author, except in the case of brief quotations embodied in critical articles and reviews.

The Author of this book is solely responsible and liable for its content including but not limited to the views, representations, descriptions, statements, information, opinions and references ["Content"]. The Content of this book shall not constitute or be construed or deemed to reflect the opinion or expression of the Publisher or Editor. Neither the Publisher nor Editor endorse or approve the Content of this book or guarantee the reliability, accuracy or completeness of the Content published herein and do not make any representations or warranties of any kind, express or implied, including but not limited to the implied warranties of merchantability, fitness for a particular purpose. The Publisher and Editor shall not be liable whatsoever for any errors, omissions, whether such errors or omissions result from negligence, accident, or any other cause or claims for loss or damages of any kind, including without limitation, indirect or consequential loss or damage arising out of use, inability to use, or about the reliability, accuracy or sufficiency of the information contained in this book.

Made with ♥ on the Notion Press Platform
www.notionpress.com

Dedicated to the tenacious students, encouraging parents, and devoted educators who are constantly striving for career excellence - this book is for you. Your tireless pursuit of success and resolute dedication to education are truly awe-inspiring. Let the insights and wisdom contained within these pages propel you to even greater heights on your career path.

May this book serve as a guiding light, helping you surmount challenges and seize opportunities. You are the visionaries and innovators of the future, and your unrelenting drive towards success is what propels us forward.

This dedication is a testament to our shared commitment to education, development, and career fulfilment. Thank you for your unwavering persistence and for being the driving force behind a brighter tomorrow.

Contents

Foreword   *vii*

Preface   *ix*

Introduction   *xi*

1. The Success Mindset Blueprint: Transforming Values,   1
   Perception, And Esteem For A Fulfilling Career And Life

2. Mastering Habits: Your Guide To Diligence, Time   22
   Management, And Daily Routines For Boosting
   Productivity And Achieving Success

3. Beyond The Classroom: How To Navigate Career Choices 50
   And Find Your Calling With A Mentor And Outside
   Perspective

4. Choosing Your Path: A Guide To Career Selection, Self-   59
   worth, And Goal Setting For A Purposeful Life

5. Study Skill: How To Read Faster And Comprehend   117
   Better, Problem With Slow Reading, Speed Reading
   Exercise

6. High-income Skills For The 21st Century: Mastering   130
   Public Speaking, Writing, Sales, And Leadership For
   Career Success

7. The Entrepreneur's Journey: Building Success In   147
   Edupreneur, Trading, Manufacturing, And More For A
   Fulfilling Life And Career

Reference List   167

About The Author   169

Bukim Growth's Resource   171

Foreword

No.7/RBC/PRIN/EXT/2023(1): I am pleased to write this foreword for the book entitled <u>"Life and Career Transformation: Mastering Your Mindset, Habits and Skills for a Fulfilling Life"</u> authored by Mr Lammuansang Tombing.

In this 21st century, we are witnessing the system and product of globalization and experiencing the rise of information technology, therefore, one needs to improve and develop one's skills and potentials to survive in our modern era.

In our country in general and in our state in particular, everyone dreams of entering government service and thus serving the country.

However, I would like to point out to the young generation that they should broaden their horizons and unleash their potential by starting a business, promoting skill development, etc. To develop such a mentality and boost self-confidence to overcome the fear of failure, this book is just the thing!

I wish the author and his team all the best for their future endeavor.

.

.

(REV. DR. KHEN P. TOMBING)
Principal
Rayburn College

Preface

When I first began my journey as a certified career counsellor, I never imagined that I would be able to help so many individuals transform their lives and careers. Over the years, I have been fortunate enough to counsel over 900 students and provide over 200 career guidance to countless others through my seminars and talks.

But I realized that there are still many individuals who may not have access to the kind of personalized guidance and support that I can provide through one-on-one counselling sessions. It was with this in mind that I decided to write this book, "Life and Career Transformation: Mastering Your Mindset, Habits, and Skills for a Fulfilling Life."

In my quest to help individuals, I spent over 3 lakhs in the past three years, acquiring 19 certifications in career counselling related courses. I believe that this investment was worthwhile, as it has equipped me with the tools and knowledge necessary to help students like never before.

Drawing from my experience and training, I aim to provide a comprehensive guide that will help individuals make positive changes in their lives and achieve their goals. Whether you are a student just starting out on your career path or a seasoned professional looking to make a change, this book is for you.

In this book, I cover a range of topics, including the Success Mindset Blueprint, Mastering Habits, and Beyond the Classroom. I also provide guidance on choosing your path, navigating career choices, and finding your calling. I share insights on high-income skills for the 21st century, entrepreneurship, and more.

Through this book, I hope to provide practical advice and strategies to help readers make positive changes in their lives. I also share insights from my own experience as a certified counsellor, providing real-world examples and success stories to help readers feel inspired and motivated.

With this book, my aim is to reach individuals who may not have the opportunity to attend one of my career guidance seminars or counselling sessions. I believe that by providing individuals with the tools they need to transform their lives and careers, we can help create a more fulfilling and successful future for everyone.

I am excited to share my knowledge and experience with you, and I hope that this book will be a valuable resource on your journey to personal and professional growth.

.

.

March 27, 2023
Lammuansang Tombing
(Author)

Introduction

Success mean different things to different people, but everyone can agree that it is something that we all want to achieve in life. Whether it is in our career, relationships, or personal growth, success is the ultimate goal that we strive for. However, achieving success is not always easy. It requires hard work, dedication, and most importantly, the right mindset.

In this book, "Life and Career Transformation: Mastering Your Mindset, Habits, and Skills for a Fulfilling Life," we will explore the blueprint for a success mindset and provide practical tools and techniques to help students achieve their goals. From transforming values and perception to mastering habits and navigating career choices, this book covers a range of topics to help students build the foundation for a fulfilling career and life.

Chapter 1, "The Success Mindset Blueprint," will help students understand the importance of having the right mindset and how to transform their values, perception, and esteem to achieve success. Chapter 2, "Mastering Habits," provides a guide to diligence, time management, and daily routines for boosting productivity and achieving success.

Chapter 3, "Beyond the Classroom," explores the importance of mentorship and outside perspectives in finding their calling and navigating career choices. Chapter 4, "Choosing Your Path," provides a guide to career selection, self-worth, and goal setting for a purposeful life.

Chapter 5, "Study Skills," will help students overcome the problem of slow reading by providing speed reading exercises and techniques for faster and better comprehension. Chapter 6, "High-Income Skills for the 21st Century," explores public speaking, writing, sales, and leadership skills that are essential for career success.

Finally, Chapter 7, "The Entrepreneur's Journey," provides insights and guidance on building success in edupreneurship, trading, manufacturing, and more for a fulfilling life and career.

This book is designed for students who want to achieve success in their academic, personal, and professional lives. It is a practical guide that provides the tools and techniques to transform their mindset, build the foundation for a fulfilling life, and achieve their goals. Whether you are a high school student, college student, or graduate student, this book will provide you with the knowledge and insights to succeed.

THE SUCCESS MINDSET BLUEPRINT: TRANSFORMING VALUES, PERCEPTION, AND ESTEEM FOR A FULFILLING CAREER AND LIFE

Being willing to pay the price is crucial for success. I have studied numerous success stories, and while learning what it takes to succeed is important, it may not be enough to guarantee your success. You must be willing to pay the necessary price to achieve your goals. Like when you go to a store, you cannot leave with the desired item unless you pay its price. But once you pay the MRP or the cost of the item, you can take it home.

In real life, most of the prices we pay are not in terms of money but rather something entirely different. Many people fail to understand this. While you can purchase anything in a store if you have the money, there are things more valuable than money that cannot be bought. Our mindset and character, for instance, can help us regenerate anything we have lost in life. Sadly, many of us fail to invest in what truly matters.

I have given over 200 free seminars to schools, colleges, children's homes, rehab centres, and many other places, but I have never received any appreciation from them. Not a single memento of gratitude has been given to me. I administered the DMIT Lifetime and psychometric test and free seminars to over 100 children in four children's homes to assess their inborn personality, intelligence, learning style, leadership style, career recommendations, and more. If I charged them, it would have cost Rs.5000 per student for the DMIT test, and for total, it would be more than 5 Lakhs. Why am I sharing this? Am I boasting or complaining them? No, I want you to see the reality. Instead of a personality development seminar or DMIT and psychometrics test, they would have treated me differently if I had given them the same amount of money which is over 5 Lakhs. I am not complaining or criticizing them. The program I conduct doesn't produce instant results. Investing in character or mindset doesn't provide instant results or make money immediately. This is why many of us fail to prioritize personal growth.

Often, we think that money is above all and do not focus on building our mindset or improving our habits and character. However, I can guarantee that you will never become a money magnet if you do not first change and develop in these areas.

As an edupreneur, I advise you to improve your worth by learning skills, building good character, and investing in personal growth before chasing money. If you chase money without first doing these things, the faster you chase money, the quicker it will slip away from you.

Whenever I tell my students that investing is the best way to grow yourself and your money, they often reply, 'I don't have the money to invest.' I then tell them that money is just one of the many things you can invest. Sometimes, investing in personal growth and skill sets can yield even better results than investing in cash.

Invest your time and energy into learning, developing your personality, and acquiring new skills. I know your parents have invested a lot of money in your education, hoping that one day you will become successful and earn more than what they spent. However, this is not always the case. Only 10-20% of graduates get a government job (the most secure job in India), but what about the remaining 80%?"

Perception of problems: This is why I am writing this book for you. The school education system has failed to secure luxurious jobs unless we belong to the top 10% of geniuses who excel in studies. In this book, I will show you how to succeed academically and in any career you choose. If you have come this far, please read this book until the end, not just once but twice, to find a solution to your current problems and modern job issues.

My simple principle is to study what successful people do and follow in their footsteps to achieve the same results. Similarly, study unsuccessful people, learn what makes them unsuccessful, and avoid doing what they do. In both ways, you will become successful. I have read many books and worked hard to get here from where I started. After applying everything that made me successful, I am here to pass it down to you. Yes, I was willing to pay the price and get the desired results. Are you ready to learn? Are you willing to unlearn? Are you willing to change yourself to reach the next level? Are you willing to leave your old self behind for a better version of yourself?

If the answer to any of the above questions is yes, continue reading. If not, don't waste your time reading this book, as it won't benefit you. But if you read with the faith that this book will transform you inside out, you'll see the results gradually over time.

It's not like purchasing something from a store, but something greater than that, which will take time to materialize.

To simplify, success has three levels, each with many steps. The three levels are creating a successful mindset, building successful habits and characters, and learning new skills or information. All these are interconnected, and focusing on building one will inevitably improve the other. However, if you learn how to navigate these levels and build yourself up in the most productive way possible, you will grow faster.

For instance, in martial arts, let's say Karate, the moment you start learning it, you must develop a calm mind and control your emotions, which is a successful mindset. Next, you must build stamina, willpower, and other successful habits. Lastly, you must learn how to balance your body, defend yourself, and attack your opponent, which involves acquiring new skills.

I will teach you about developing a successful mindset first and foremost.

Mindset is a choice.

1) Positive mindset: In a village in Africa, an old man was always happy and positive throughout his life. He was never known to be angry or sad. One day, all of his villagers came to him and asked for his secret to happiness. He replied that there is no secret to happiness. It was a habit for him to be happy and positive in his life.

He blessed his children, grandchildren, plants, and animals when he woke up. He blessed everyone who happened to pass by and never spoke a bad word nor had a negative attitude toward any person. He deliberately made the conscious decision to be positive and made it a habit. See, happiness is not something we have to search for and find; it is something that we must constantly choose.

I suffered from typhoid for two months, which resulted in depression. Being young and lacking guidance on mental health, I endured seven months without medication until my teachers and relatives noticed my weakened behaviour. Despite my efforts, I couldn't change my negative thoughts, and my mind refused to sleep, causing headaches and digestive issues. At that moment, I had lost hope of recovering from my depression. I hit rock bottom, feeling cursed from birth and a burden on everyone, losing control of my life. I can tell you now, 4 out of 5 happiness and successes I got in life were after my depression.

Every positive has the potential to create something good, and every negative has the potential to destroy something good. For example, love is a positive emotion that creates something good if you love someone. You feel good about yourself and have a good mood when in love, making you energetic and productive. Within a few weeks, you will start to consciously or unconsciously do and say good things to the person you love, which creates something good in the other person.

On the other hand, if you hate someone, hate is a negative emotion that destroys something good. You may knowingly or unknowingly hurt the person you hate, and your negativity will ruin not only your own good nature and also the lives of others. You will start to lose your good mood and motivation for work, and your negative mindset will eventually show outwardly.

To the person reading this book, if you are experiencing depression, I understand that it may be difficult to believe and consume these ideas. However, I want you to know that I have been where you are right now, and 4/5 of my happiness and success came after my depression. The ideas I am about to share with you are the things that helped me break through my depression. So, I encourage you to continue reading.

In short, if you want to build something up, don't hate it; you have already destroyed it by hating it. If you're going to build yourself up or other people, don't hate or have a negative mindset. Only with the right mindset and a positive heart can you improve and build something good in life.

2) Mind Gardener:
We are all gardeners, even if we are not farmers or do not have a plot of land to grow plants. But we are all gardeners of our own

minds. Every day, we face both good and bad situations, but we hardly make a conscious decision about whether to stay in a good or bad mood. Our mood is controlled by our environment. When we experience something good, we are happy. If we face something bad, we are sad. There is no conscious decision about which side we should choose.

Believe me, if someone can make you angry every time, even with little things, it means that you are emotionally a slave to that person. Don't allow situations or bad people to take away your good and positive mindset. We have to control our mood and consciously decide to stay positive.

To be successful, we have to be mindful. Like a gardener, we must choose which seeds we will plant in our garden (mind). If we don't consciously plant good seeds, thorns and nettles will grow, which are useless and have no value in our lives. We must only grow fruits that bring value and benefits to us, our families, and everyone around us.

What we sow in our mind, we will reap in life. Plant good ideas to benefit you, your family, and your community.

3) Mind Factory Owners:

As a mind factory owner, your mind is like a factory where whatever ideas you put in will be manifested in your life. Using your mind as a dustbin will soon create a bad smell, and nothing of value will come out. Only put great and positive thoughts into your mind. Believe me, if you put the idea that you are useless, gradually, you will become ineffective in real life as your inner voice is acted out and reflected in your behaviour.

Just as a shoe manufacturer wouldn't make shoes that are too small or too large because they would have no customers to buy them, your mind is like a manufacturing machine. Don't put in ideas that will hurt yourself or others. Instead, focus on ideas that will help you grow, build you up, and motivate you to work harder.

4) Mind Architecture:

If I gave you 80 Lakh rupees to build your house, who would instantly start building without a design and without seeking help from an architect? But have you ever considered that your life is much more valuable than an 80 lakh rupee building? Have you even ever tried to build up your life? When was the last time you wrote down your life goal and really tried to become successful in life? When was the last time you tried to design your life like an architect's plans and designs a building?

You can't change other people's lives, how they feel about you, or their destination. But you can plan and change your life through proper planning and designing, and if God blesses your work, then success will follow. But if you never plan or work towards success, there is nothing left for God to bless. Plan, work, and hope for blessings instead of just hoping for blessings to change your life.

If you are feeling stuck in life, without a sense of purpose and thinking that you are worthless, stop for a moment and ask yourself about your goals, future plans, and efforts. You may have never planned or set a goal in life, which may be the reason why you've lost your sense of identity. As humans, we have a sense of purpose and identify ourselves through our work. To build your life, develop your career.

Why we need to change our mindset:

a.

Life script

Fruit doesn't fall far from the tree. Till the age of two years, we absorbed emotions and everything from our parents and family environment. Yes, we take in everything without our conscious mind; it is not up to us whether to consume. We are still innocent and can't make a decision for ourselves. We absorb all emotions if our parents keep fighting and release a negative environment.

They are like emotional sponges. We don't understand their word and meaning or why they argue. But as a child, we think everything happens through us, and for us, we are 100% emotional and 0% rational. We are self-centred. Our parents may not be mad at us, or the reason why they shout may not include us, but still, we absorb those emotions that fly in our environment.

Why am I telling you all this? It is because our life script is written before we can decide for ourselves. It is based on our family environment. The life script is something very hard to rewrite. If you are depressed most of the time, you must rewrite your life script. All our personality and character are what we collect from our childhood, most of them without making a conscious decision. Many of us think that we were born this way, and some believe it is unchangeable, even if our habits or character are not successful. Wherever we are right now is our comfort zone, and many of us are unwilling to change, even if it's for the better.

All successful people have changed their life scripts through a painful process, which led them to successful habits and characteristics. It is very hard to change in a comfortable life, but when we are depressed and dislike ourselves, we crave change. That's the best time to change our life script. Mine was changed during my depression, and I achieved greater things after that. Of course, I don't suggest anyone to become depressed. But if you are, take the opportunity to change your life script. Some depressed individuals can't take advantage of their depression, which saddens me. Depression is when we feel we've lost everything, which gives us an opportunity to start a new life. Intensity and self-hatred can be powerful tools to build a successful new life, character, habits, and personality.

Yes, depression is not the only way to change our life script or the best opportunity. The best practice and the best chance come when we try something great and get stuck. Unless we become a better version of ourselves, we cannot achieve our goals. That's the best opportunity and way to change our life script. When we fail at something, don't just be sad. It's the way the universe tells us that we need a better strategy or plan to become a better version of ourselves to succeed in this field. It's the best honest feedback ever."

a. Mind programming:

We human beings are like computers. Whatever input we provide, the computer system will function accordingly. The computer will only operate based on its system and will only be useful according to its programming. Similarly, humans have our first mind programming before the age of 7, and for some of us, that programming remains unchanged. This is one of the reasons why many of us don't achieve the success we are capable of.

We are still emotional kids during those early years and do not choose our own mind system. Our first mind program is built based on our environment and our family. It is given to us, and we have no choice. Because of this programming, we function daily and live our lives. But if you want greater success and achievement in life, it is compulsory to change your mindset.

This is why some men exhibit childish behaviour even after becoming adults. Those who are too emotional and self-centred still function based on their first mind program. As a child, we need care and love, but to be successful in our careers and life, we also need to be tough and bold. These traits may be included to some extent in our initial programming, but a large portion may be missing. Therefore, when we try to be disciplined and hardworking, we encounter difficulties because, before age 7, these traits were not emphasized in our mental programming. So, if you want to achieve success and fulfilment in life, you must consciously change your mindset and programming.

How to cultivate a new mindset

1) Continuously feeding the idea

While our physical abilities have remained relatively unchanged over the past 3000 years, our mental capacities continue to be explored and tested to this day. Our minds have the power to make a ton of metal float on water, to make a ton of metal fly in the sky, and to make our voices audible and our faces visible from a thousand miles away. Of course, God is behind everything else, but I am only comparing our human capacities here.

A single idea has the power to change everything, but we must continuously feed it into our minds every day until the idea becomes visible to us. Take Henry Ford, for example. He only attended school for eight years in his lifetime. Although there were already vehicles during his time, they did not have fast engines.

When he first shared with his engineers that he would create a new engine faster than before, all his engineers laughed at him and told him that it was impossible to make such an engine. But he persisted and kept feeding the idea and fuelling his dream. After five years, those same engineers who had said it was impossible ended up inventing the engine.

Thomas A. Edison made our modern electric bulb and was not a college graduate. He tried to improve it to shine like our normal modern bulb and tried over 10,000 times before finally accomplishing it. He was a persistent man who kept fuelling his dream by continuously suggesting ideas in his mind and believing his work would someday be successful. During his time, there was already an electric current and a beam light bulb which is used in the present day as an electric gate bulb.

During my 11th-grade class, one of my English teachers said, "To not be forgotten after death for 100 years, you must do one big thing for the community or write a book." From there, I wanted to become an author and promised to write three books before completing my graduate degree. I bought some paper and began writing, but after two pages, I got lost and didn't know what else to write or how to continue. It felt like a nightmare, and it seemed impossible to fulfil my goal.

I was very bad at my studies during high school, failing three or four subjects out of six in most exams. My grammar was weak, and I didn't even have the habit of writing. But I continued to fuel my idea, and by my third year of college, I knew I had promised to complete three books before graduating.

On September 30th, I attended a webinar, "How to complete a book in 30 days." There, I learned that my dream was not so far-fetched, and I believed in their teaching and started writing my first book. Wonderfully, I completed my first draft within six days. After about three weeks of editing, we finally published it, and my first book sold 900 copies in the first month. I wrote two more books before completing my graduate degree.

At first, our dream and goal may seem unrealistic and impossible, and that is okay. Yes, it was impossible for me to complete a book in 11th grade, but it was possible within five years. Nobody knows how I would improve or what skills I would acquire in that time. We all start our dreams with something unrealistic and impossible, but we should never give up.

Keep fuelling your idea in your head persistently until your dreams become true. Nobody knows the future, and you may not have what it takes to become successful the moment you set a goal. If you already have the skills and have succeeded, that won't be your dream anymore. When developing a goal, you know you don't have the necessary skills or knowledge, but as long as you are willing to learn and grow, you'll achieve them. Like my best friend used to say, "I don't know when or how I will succeed, but I definitely know that someday I will be successful."

We have discussed the importance of persistence and continuously suggesting ideas to ourselves every day. Now let's talk about how to do it exactly:

To start with, we need to understand the concept of change. All change begins with new or old information with a different level of experience. This new information or experience will change our perspective toward life, and we will react to it by trying to improve ourselves, resulting in slight or significant behavioural changes.

To create a significant change in our lives, we must repeatedly feed this new idea or perspective into our heads for at least 11 weeks. If we are disciplined and manage to feed the new concept and make changes in our behaviour for a minimum of 11 weeks, then this mindset and behaviour will become our habit. We will function with the new mind program, knowingly or unknowingly, which will bring new results in our exams, relationships, or environments.

Many of us can't keep up with the 11 weeks and can't cultivate new habits, falling back into our comfort zones. To keep ourselves committed to creating new habits or being successful in our careers, we need to make these ideas the dominant thoughts in our brains. We will talk more about this in the next chapter.

2) Asking Others to Support You

Many of us fear sharing our dreams and goals with others, thinking, "What if I don't succeed? What if I want to change my goal later? If I share my goal with others, my secret will not be safe, and someone else may plan to let me down?" These thoughts are normal, and there is a secure way to share our dreams and an insecure way that we must avoid. There are also many benefits to sharing our goals with someone else. Let me first tell you with whom you should share your dream.

The first rule is to never share your dream in public or with someone who does not have a goal. They may think it is useless, and some negative people will try to talk you out of your dream because it seems impossible for them to achieve what you tried to do. They will speak to you from their level of mindset and willpower.

Secondly, never share your dream with negative people. It may be someone close to you, but if their mindset is negative, do not share it with them. I once shared my dream with my grandfather, and he talked to me as if I was worthless. He completely destroyed my self-esteem just because he could not see my potential and the qualifying nature of the job.

But it would be best to share your dream and goal with certain people.

First, share it with your mentor or someone you consult when making big decisions. They should know your plan because, with this knowledge, they will be able to guide you better in all areas of life. They can even give you better advice about your current goal.

Secondly, share it with your best friend, but they should be a positive person who can support you and offer emotional support. Do not share it with people not close to you because if you change your goal later, you will need to update the information. Otherwise, they might think of you as a failure for not being able to achieve the goal that you changed.

Thirdly, you cannot keep a secret from your parents. You cannot keep it a secret and expect support from them. Your parents are your decision-makers until you are mature enough to make your own decisions. They will decide which school or college you should attend and which stream or subject you should study. So, sharing your dreams and goals with your parents is very important.

Some benefits of sharing your dreams include receiving feedback, suggestions, red flags, encouragement, prayer, and even financial support in the long run.

As an extroverted person who loves sharing my dreams, I have shared my dreams with many others and received plenty of advice, feedback, and suggestions. At one point, I shared my two-year project plan with one of my counsellor's friends. He provided me with practical and deeper information about my project, which I was trying to do in the near future. He told me that the chances of success were only 0.1%, based on his experience and the mindset and attitudes of the public. Before embarrassing myself, I decided to take precautions and postpone the project until later.

When seeking advice, it is essential to approach someone older and wiser than you, who continuously reads books and updates themselves in their field. Try your best to find the right person, not just someone like your grandfather, who is not related and unaware of your topic.

Whenever a king needs advice about his kingdom, he never consults a beggar or blacksmith. He always surrounds himself with the wisest and most educated people in his land and takes the recommendations of his most trusted advisers. This doesn't mean you must take all their suggestions and be affected by other opinions. But for me, this person is someone whom I really trust. He has 15 years of experience in the field in which I am trying to work, has all the connections, and knows the nature and attitudes of those I was trying to seek sponsorships and help from. If I didn't take his advice, I would be foolish.

On another occasion, I happened to share my future goals with one of my mentors, who is a pastor. Of course, he didn't have many suggestions since he was not that aware of my topic. But the good thing is that he stood up and encouraged me, and before I left, he said a word of prayer. This was something that I hardly got from any other person. My mind was peaceful and happy to hear that my dreams were watered with prayer. I have more confidence in the plans and goals which I made for myself, knowing that God knows them and will lead and support me in all my ways until I achieve success.

New Successful Mindset

1.

High Self-esteem

Having high self-esteem is crucial. Every human has a certain level of self-worth that defines how they perceive themselves. This self-worth determines the worth of all other things in their life. While some individuals are wise and intelligent, their low self-esteem often prevents them from dreaming big. In contrast, some less intelligent people dare to dream big and achieve high levels of success in life. This shows that our mindset, not our inborn talent or family background, determines our destination. However, I don't mean to say that talent isn't essential for success. But what type of success or in what area you can achieve success is highly dependent on your level of self-esteem.

If you want to assess your self-esteem, ask yourself which options you would choose: "King or subject?" "Leader or follower?" "Rich or poor?" "Hero or loser?" and "Risk or comfort?"

Low self-esteem individuals would typically choose to be among the subjects over becoming a king or a follower instead of a leader. Why? Because they have a low sense of self-worth and never think that they are capable of achieving greatness. While you may have accomplished nothing significant up to this point, if you believe you are worth much, you can still become someone great in the future.

Individuals with low self-esteem often put themselves below others and lack confidence in their lives. Let me tell you a story that has always inspired me. There was a cat-fighting competition held all over the world. After many rounds, only three cats remained: the USA Cat, the India Cat, and the Somalia Cat. More than half of the audience supported the USA Cat since it was a superpower nation, while the rest supported the India Cat. Nobody believed in the Somalia Cat and had no supporters. Somalia is a small and one of the poorest countries.

Contrary to what most people believe, the Somalia Cat won over the USA Cat and India Cat and was awarded the medal and trophy. This shocked everyone and the media asked the Somalia Cat how he defeated the two most powerful countries competing against him. When the Somalia Cat heard this, he stood up and said, surprisingly, "Don't you see that I am a Tiger?"

No matter where you are in life, having high self-esteem always puts you ahead of achieving something great. But if you have low self-esteem, even if you have the skills and talent to become great, you will never get far from the limitations you set for yourself. You won't dare to do great things, and your potential and talent will be wasted. Change your low self-esteem into a high self-esteem mindset.

In life, what you give to yourself is what you receive. So, only give yourself what is good, best, and worthy. If you are not a leader, somebody else will hold that position. If you constantly give yourself the worst, within a matter of months, you will become depressed. Our emotions are like children; we need to give them good nourishment for them to grow. If you always keep yourself at the bottom and believe that everyone else is better than you, you will lose motivation and work less than most people, leading to the worst-case scenario.

There was a beggar who sat near the roadside. This beggar was not a born beggar. Before the Second World War, he was a multi-millionaire, but his factories and everything were destroyed by bombs, and he went bankrupt. His wife and children left him, and he became depressed and an alcoholic, and he has not worked since then. Three months had already passed, and he begged near that roadside.

One evening, one of his multi-millionaire friends, whose company had not been destroyed by the war and was still the CEO of that company, happened to walk by that road. The beggar called him and introduced himself, saying, "Friend, do you still know me? I am that multi-millionaire who owns the XYZ company, but due to this Second World War, all my industry and property have been destroyed, and now I have become a beggar. Please help me. I have many problems to solve, and even my family has left me. I need a job. Please give me a job under your company."

His friend replied, "Yes, I remember you now. Come to my office tomorrow at 10 AM, and I will show you someone who can help you with all your troubles."

The beggar was so happy that he could not sleep, even at night, when he heard that he would meet someone who could solve all his problems.

The next morning, he went to his friend's office excitedly. He couldn't even sit still and wait for his friend to introduce him to this person who could solve all his problems. So, he grabbed his friend's hand and said, "Show me this man whom you mentioned yesterday, the one who can solve all my problems. I want to see him now."

As he was reluctant to let go of his hand, the multi-millionaire friend stood up and brought him into one big room, and he let the beggar stand in front of a big curtain. He told the beggar that whoever he saw was the person who could help him out of all his problems and turn him (the beggar) into a multi-millionaire again, and reaffirmed that he must believe in him. The beggar replied, "Yes, whoever, big or small, ugly or handsome, man or woman, whoever I see, I will believe that he has the solution to all my problems and will put my trust in him. Now, show me."

After hearing this, the multi-millionaire friend pulls down the big, tall curtain, revealing a large mirror on the other side. When the bagger saw himself in the mirror, he realized that he was not born into a rich family. He worked hard and started a small business, growing slowly over 15 years to become a multi-millionaire. But due to the wars, all his companies were destroyed. Nevertheless, he was still the same person who had made himself a multi-millionaire. He was 100% responsible for all his problems and the only person who could solve them and turn himself from a beggar into a millionaire.

After reflecting on his life in the mirror, he had tears in his eyes that fell down his cheeks. He turned to his friend, hugged him, and thanked him for showing him who he was and what he could do. He told him he wouldn't take the job; instead, he would return and start a business from ground zero. True to his word, he started a business and many years later, the multi-millionaire saw him near the beach, where he had his family and bodyguards.

2. Money

Whether you are rich or poor, it doesn't matter. Your perspective on money should be right. If you have a wrong mindset regarding money, it will be very hard to attract it and easy to lose it. Most poor people would say, "Money is not everything, it is the root of all evil." When asked about their future, they'll say, "I don't want to be rich; it's enough if I could support my family."

This is a selfish attitude. Dr APJ Abdul Kalam once said that having a small dream is a sin and a bad attitude for our country. Imagine if all your community members had no big dreams and only wanted to do easy work and get paid instantly. Your community would be unable to sustain itself and would lack many skills and resources. Imagine the consequences if all of your community members work in a brick field, imagine the consequences? It would lack skills such as electricians, plumbers, administrators, and many other things.

The truth is that lazy people avoid big dreams, which require a lot of effort, attention, and hard work for many years. There is a high risk of failure, and these people don't want risk; they want comfort. They don't want to work for many years and have no patience; they want money and results instantly. Of course, we all have our callings, and one has to work according to their calling, whether big or small, little or more salary, comfort or discomfort is another thing. But here, I am talking about the people who are called to something big but choose a career that is not their calling. We will discuss this more in chapter 4.

Money itself is not a sin; it is just a tool to be used. Money manifests our true nature, and we shouldn't blame the tool. Success and money often come together like two sides of the same coin. Of course, in some cases, this may not be applied, such as religious matters. But other than that, see any success, fame and money will always follow. In the Bible, God asks Solomon, "Ask me anything, and I will give it to you." Solomon asks God for wisdom to lead his people, not gold or fame. Still, God gave him lots of gold and fame as well.

Please don't choose a career based on salary; later on, you'll regret it. A career should be selected based on your calling. In whatever you do, try to be the best among all. And when money comes, don't panic. It's not your ultimate goal, but a very powerful tool to boost your career and help your family and the needy. Don't be a slave to money; follow your passion and work hard to be at the top of your field. And expect money; plan ahead on how to spend, save, and use it. Those who are not mentally prepared for big money are the ones who mostly waste and misuse it.

Observe any person who got rich by luck. I have heard of someone who got 10 million in Lucky draw and wasted it in 3 months. Search on YouTube, and there will be many stories related to this. It shows us that we must prepare our minds on how to handle big money.

In short, success and money often come together, so if you are prepared to be successful, be prepared to handle big money so that it won't consume you and destroy your career.

3) Success

Success is not a destination but a journey. Try to enjoy the preparation for your career, and don't isolate yourself from the rest of the world just because you want to study. If you love the journey, you won't feel like your destination is far away. The people who succeed are not the ones who only desire success but those who enjoy the process of preparation. Here, "enjoy" doesn't mean avoiding working and doing other things for pleasure. It means you shouldn't avoid the journey and preparation because you don't enjoy them.

Take a moment to reflect: Do you really love the journey? Are you willing to invest the time needed to be successful? Do you enjoy the preparation and not avoid it? Can you make the preparation more interesting and enjoyable? Will you regret preparing for this career if you don't achieve success?

What does success mean to you? Be clear about your WHY and HOW; the task will not be difficult. When our "why" is not clear, our motivation weakens, and our efforts towards the goal diminish.

Cognitive Restructuring

Challenging Negative Thought Patterns to Improve Well-Being

Cognitive restructuring involves identifying and questioning negative thoughts, beliefs, and assumptions that contribute to negative emotions and behaviours. Through this process, individuals can learn to replace negative thoughts with more balanced and accurate ones. Here are some common types of cognitive distortions that cognitive restructuring can help address, along with examples:

1. **All-or-Nothing Thinking:** This is also called black-and-white thinking, where individuals view situations in extreme terms of good or bad, with no middle ground. For example, a student might think that they have completely failed unless they receive an A on an exam, ignoring the possibility of receiving a B or a C.
2. **Overgeneralization:** This involves making sweeping conclusions based on a single event or piece of evidence. For example, a person might assume that they are unlovable because they were rejected by one person in the past.
3. **Mental Filtering:** This involves selectively focusing on negative aspects of a situation while ignoring positive ones. For example, a person might overlook their accomplishments in a particular area and focus only on their shortcomings.
4. **Personalization:** This involves taking things personally and assuming that negative events are a reflection of our worth as individuals. For example, a person might feel hurt and rejected when someone cancels plans with them, assuming that it must be because they are not likeable or not interesting enough when in reality, the other person might be dealing with their own personal issues and has nothing to do with them.
5. **Catastrophizing:** This involves exaggerating the significance of negative events and imagining the worst-case scenarios. For example, a person might assume they will never find love after a break-up or fail at everything if they make a mistake.
6. **Mind Reading:** This involves assuming that we know what others think or feel without evidence supporting our beliefs. For example, a person might assume their boss is angry with them because they were not invited to a meeting, even though they have no evidence to support this assumption.

7. **Labelling:** involves attaching negative labels to ourselves or others based on past behaviours or mistakes. For example, a person might label themselves as a "failure" because they did not meet a specific goal, ignoring the progress they have made and the potential for future success.

8. **Should and Must Statements:** These are rigid and unrealistic rules we create for ourselves that can cause guilt or anxiety when we don't live up to them. For example, a person might tell themselves that they should never make mistakes or that they must always please everyone, leading to feelings of self-doubt and anxiety.

Through cognitive restructuring, individuals can learn to identify these types of negative and distorted thought patterns and challenge them with more realistic and balanced thoughts. This process can lead to reduced negative emotions and behaviours, improved coping skills, and a greater sense of well-being.

CHAPTER TWO

Mastering Habits: Your Guide to Diligence, Time Management, and Daily Routines for Boosting Productivity and Achieving Success

Diligence is one of the most crucial qualities to consider in all aspects. God never calls someone lazy to do his work; even Satan can't use a lazy person. The community praises hardworking individuals, not the lazy. Laziness is the best way to destroy your life and career, as it deteriorates all aspects of life. Diligence or laziness is not a one-time action but a habit that can be cultivated and considered an asset.

One of the reasons why our community has become lazier is that we forget to train our children to be diligent. Lots of love and care can lead to self-pettiness if not given correctly. Love and care are essential for nurturing our kids, but excessive care can lead to many problems. One of the parents must be strict, and the other must have a kind heart as much as possible.

If both parents are too strict or too soft together, problems can arise for their children when they grow up. If both parents are strict, the children can suffer from emotional issues. If both parents are soft, the children can lack confidence and become overly dependent on others. These are only a few parenting issues; if you want to read more about parenting, check out from time to time, I will be writing a parenting book in the near future.

The other reason could be that we did not change our life script and mind programming, which were created while we were still children, and it was easier to mould those days. But now that we have grown up, those life scripts and mind programming, which were built softly, need to be changed to achieve higher success.

If your parents are strict and educated, they are more likely to shape you into a diligent person. If not, you have to consciously make an effort to become diligent. When we are young, we want comfort and don't value hardship. Everything has to be comfortable, and they can't handle even a little hardship. But now, we are wiser and more mature than ever before. It is up to us to decide whether to stay lazy and not become successful in life or to build ourselves up and cultivate new habits, such as diligence or hard work, to become part of the top 1% of super-successful people.

To be successful, we have to be mindful. I consciously decided to become diligent, and everything changed from that moment onward. Before September 2018, I was not active in my work. Of course, since my childhood, I have loved learning and studying new things. I enrolled in martial arts and practised for 5 years, earning a black belt in 8th grade. I learned a lot of things, but I was lazy when it came to housework, such as washing clothes and helping others physically.

One day, I read about the benefits of being diligent and discovered that diligence (hard work) is a common quality among all the most successful people. From then on, I made a strong commitment to make diligence a new habit and not hesitate to do any work required to be successful. The next morning, I started washing my clothes, not just mine, but my mother and brother clothing. I began ploughing the garden, worked as a "Jugali" in the construction of a building, and also helped my relatives, who were about 8 family members, by washing their clothes, as all the women were sick and couldn't wash for 2 weeks.

I changed my mindset and stopped looking for rewards or money; my objective is to cultivate the new habit of diligence. For me, having work is an opportunity, not a burden. Lazy person carries a lot of hurdles because they keep delaying their work, and after a long time, there is too much work to be done at once.

People with high IQs are usually more organized and diligent than most people. When we are active and work hard, our relationship with our family improves, and they don't need to scold or push us to work. We receive praise, which motivates us to work more, and we are respected and loved because we are organized and look fresh. When we look organized and attractive, we look more like educated people.

When you develop the habit of diligence, you become more mature in taking responsibility, achieve better grades, and become more attractive to others. There is a very low chance for others to look down on you. If you do your duty, no higher authority can punish you. When you perform your part to the best of your ability, no one has the right to scold you. If you make diligence a habit, your value will increase to double and triple then now. You will have a higher chance of success than ever before, and others will be more willing to help you when you get into trouble. A lazy person cannot be helped, but helping a diligent person once lasts forever.

Set your mind straight and commit yourself, no matter how tough, difficult, or changing it gets. I won't go back to my lazy habits and will work my tail off once and for all. I hereby commit myself to do anything for three months straight. Why three months?

Cultivating a New Habit

Cultivating a new habit or breaking an old one requires only 11 to 13 weeks. If you acquire a new habit, you can succeed in any field. Most failures are caused by our habits, although when people fail, they blame the situation, people or themselves. Only a few people blame their habits. However, when you blame your habit for failure, change those ineffective daily habits, and replace them with more successful ones, the results will vary.

What is tough? Is it not having the habit or doing the work? For those who don't have the habit of studying for five hours a day, studying for five hours in a single day will be very tough. However, it will be just another normal day for someone who has the habit. Is waking up at 5AM tough? No, only if you don't have the habit. A present-day teenager who wakes up at 8AM will find it very difficult to wake up at 5AM, but for an army personnel who has the habit of waking up at 4AM, it is not too difficult to wake up at 5AM. Therefore, why something is tough might not be the real reason it is tough.

Everything about you - the way you walk, talk, sound, the words you use, your success or failure - is due to your habits (subconscious mind) which make up 95% of who you are and who you become. This subconscious mind (habit) consists of 95% of who you are and what you'll become in the future. If you learn to control your subconscious mind, achieving any goal or dream won't be that hard.

What you think is tough is not the real challenge but the habit-building process that makes it tough. Anything that is not your habit will be tough for you until that behaviour becomes your habit. Once an action becomes a habit, the toughness and difficulties are gone because of the realization of the conscious mind (5%), which controls your subconscious mind.

Any idea or action that you encounter every day first enters your conscious mind. When you repeatedly think about it, it becomes the dominant thought in your mind. Anything that is the dominant thought in our mind becomes something we consciously or unconsciously act out.

It is so tough to do something for the first time due to the adjustment of our mind and body. The more often you do it, the more adjusted you become and the easier it becomes. As it becomes easier, it shifts faster from the conscious into the subconscious mind. The toughness and difficulties we face are due to our conscious mind pushing us to do something unfamiliar and uncomfortable. Adjusting from comfort to discomfort is tough, but once pain becomes our comfort zone, it is easy and no longer needs adjusting, and the conscious mind can relax and be taken over by the subconscious mind.

The more you think of something, the more you act on it, and the more you repeatedly think and act, the more it becomes a habit. Good or bad habits follow the same pattern. Even drug addicts find it hard at the beginning, so they start with the lowest dose, and it goes up again and again until they reach the top, and low doses are no longer effective. It is very tough the first time you wake up at 5AM, but the longer you wake up early, the easier it gets. After forming a habit of waking up at 5 AM, try sleeping until 9AM in the morning, and it will be tough again.

I tested this myself. While I was in class 11, I read a book about the power of habit. From there, I tried to implement it in my life. I strongly committed to following it continuously for at least 3 months. I decided to study for 10 hours a day. If an IAS aspirant can study for 14-16 hours a day, why can't we do the same? This thought really challenged me.

The first day I began studying for 10 hours, it was 100% tough. I didn't get enough sleep, my eyes were red during the day, and I was sleepy all the class period. I had to sit up late, study until midnight, and wake up at 5 AM. I find it hard to remember what I learned, and sometimes I am angry at myself. After the first week, it was the toughest (80% toughness), I had to adjust my sleep, but my willpower had to be strong. I had to be more disciplined than ever before. I suffered temporary pain to gain a new habit of studying for 10 hours every day, and it was worth it.

After one month, it becomes easier (50% toughness), and after two months, it becomes 30% tough, and finally, after three months, the difficulty becomes normal (0% toughness). I don't have to use my conscious mind to push myself to wake up early or force myself to study. Without much awareness, I keep studying for 10 hours every day after the 3 months.

I know students find it hard to study for even 2 hours, but I urge you to study every day for at least 5 hours consciously for 3 months. See whether it is too difficult to study for 2 hours every day. Your grades will automatically improve, and you won't have to stress about exams or learning notes. Your friends will admire you, and your teachers will appreciate you. Your self-esteem will boost, and your confidence level will rise. Your parents will be proud of you. In high school, I used to fail in 3/6 of subjects, but once I cultivated the habit of studying for 10 hours a day, my grades went up, and I scored mostly among the top 5 out of 400 students from Section A to Section E at Rayburn College, Churachandpur.

Don't think it's impossible for you; commit yourself for 3 months straight. Change your classroom environment and gain respect from your peers. I have done it, and it's very possible. In class 12, I studied for 12 hours a day. Of course, there were off days, and nobody was perfect. You can rest on some nights. But don't quit, and even if you are going to take a break, don't do it before you complete 3 months, or else you can't form it into a habit.

Try it out and share your results with me through my email (bukimgrowth@gmail.com). Your stories can become an inspiration for many others.

How to push yourself

1. **Commitment:** Your discipline should be based on commitment, not emotion. If you base your discipline on emotion, you will only study when you feel like it. And if you only study when you feel like it or according to your interest, you will never develop the habit. Base your discipline on commitment. If you set a goal to study for 5 hours a day, do it anyway, regardless of your emotions, which can fluctuate. Never let your commitment waver. Commitment is steady and firm. The benefits are in your hands if you can study continuously for 3 months without quitting. Be willing to pay the price. Don't worry whether your mind is sharp or your results improve. Just focus on building the habit. Once you create the habit, the rest of the benefits will follow. This doesn't mean you have to quit after 3 months. It only means that the toughness will not be as challenging, and you'll be able to study for longer hours more easily.

2. **Self-affirmation:** This is one hundred per cent compulsory for the first 3 months. This is the only way to make conscious, dominant thoughts in your mind. If you can't make your new habit idea the dominant thought, you won't be able to form the habit. Because the less you think, the less you do, and the less you do, the less likely the habit is to form. Now, how to do this? What to say in self-affirmation?

"I am proud of myself for dedicating 5 hours daily to my studies. I see positive results in my grades and recognition from my teachers, parents, and even my friends. My hard work and discipline have transformed my life, and I am filled with a sense of fulfillment and joy as I continue to grow and succeed."

Lie down on your bed just before you go to sleep. Close your eyes and visualize your plan; the next morning will be easier to wake up and study. Visualize and assume that you have achieved your goal and how your life will change. While you think about all of this, fall asleep. Our subconscious mind works best when we visualize just before sleeping. Whatever we think before sleep goes deep into our subconscious mind. The next morning won't be as challenging as your mind is already prepared.

As soon as you wake up in the morning, just before you get out of bed, visualize again, but not for too long. One or two minutes is enough. Before bed, do it for 10-15 minutes, and don't worry about falling asleep. While you dream about your future, sleep on it.

During the day, when you are alone, you may or may not close your eyes. It depends on you. Think the same idea, and as much as possible, try to let this idea dominate your mind. Let it be your dominant thought for at least three months straight. The more this idea dominates your thoughts, the more likely you are to act on it. Fuel your thoughts with motivation to help prepare your conscious mind for the work ahead. Remember that clarity is a must; your dialogue should not be in the future tense or passive. It must be active and in the present tense.

Whether you are Christian or not, you can still apply this in your prayers. Pray as clearly and emotionally as possible. Believe in the power of God to change you, and pray with faith.

3. **One step at a time:** If you have strong willpower, you can start by directly studying for 5 hours a day. However, if you are a soft person without a strong will, don't start with 5 hours immediately. It may become your stumbling block and cause embarrassment. If you haven't had proper study hours and routines and hardly study at night, follow this one-step-at-a-time approach. Start small, but it should still be challenging. Don't plan for just one hour because it's too short, and even if you manage to study for one hour, you won't be happy. If you want to start small, begin with 3 hours in the first week, add another hour in the second week to make it 4 hours, add another hour in the third week, and maintain a 5-hour study habit for 3 months straight. It won't motivate you to do more if it's not challenging, even when you achieve it. So be bold. If you're scared, it means

it's worth trying.

4. **Self-pity:** You must learn to reward and treat yourself with respect and proper care. But don't fall into a self-pity mood; it will weaken you and make you a failure in life. When your mind says, "It's too cold to get up" or "I didn't get enough sleep and need to sleep more," reply to those thoughts with ", I won't die of cold, but if I continue to sleep, I won't be successful in life. So, I must get up" and "It's not that big a problem to not get enough sleep for just one night. It's manageable. I will wake up." Self-pity is the disease of depression, so don't indulge in it unless you want to invite depression into your life.

5. **Reward yourself:** You must learn to reward and treat yourself with respect and proper care. Our emotions are like children, and the more you take good care of them, the more they will obey you. Don't only criticize yourself when you make a mistake; learn to appreciate yourself when you do something good. If it's something challenging, learn to reward yourself. Like any person in an office, no great work can be expected without appreciation and reward. The same goes for you, don't expect motivation and success if you can't appreciate yourself even when others don't appreciate you.

Any organization that lacks appreciation and reward will have many disputes among its members, and they won't be productive. The same thing applies to you; when you lack appreciation and reward for yourself, you start complaining and have many internal issues. Your motivation will decrease, and you won't be productive. So, from time to time, learn to appreciate yourself and treat yourself to your favourite snack or meal when you've completed a challenging task. If you get tired, rest. Rest is not an act of laziness. Lazy people don't get tired of working but keep resting continuously. Diligent people work hard and rest according to their needs, not just because they want to rest but because they need rest. Ask yourself, "Do you only rest when you need it or whenever you want it?"

Extra Mile

The simplest way to become extraordinary is to work extra more than anyone else. Students who study like students and not like their professors will always be ordinary students. The way our teachers study and prepare for our syllabus and the pattern we do are not the same. Teachers look beyond their syllabus, collect relevant information from other sources, and read and study beyond our syllabus to explain with more clarity and facts. But we, as students, check only the notes given by our teachers and the school subjects, which makes us limited and inferior to our teachers.

As soon as I finished my class 11 exams, I bought the class 12 textbook and began studying. Before my class 11 results came out, I had covered half of my class 12 political science syllabus, and when we started our class, I had already finished 18 out of the 20 chapters. Attending class was like revision for me; things I couldn't understand while studying alone, and I could clear my doubts in class.

When we don't study our syllabus before class, we don't have many questions to ask because everything is new, and we're confident that once we read it, we can understand it. But later on, when we can't understand the subject, there are few opportunities to clear our doubts because the chapter has already changed and a new lesson has started.

You don't need to depend on class teaching if you can read the syllabus. There are no rules, such as not to cover the syllabus on your own and waiting until our teacher explains it. If you're taking science and math, it might be good to wait for the explanation first, but for the rest of the subjects, you can read them alone.

Sometimes, if you are not careful, the school system may give you an education but not teach you successful character traits. If you depend on your teacher for everything and never try to work independently, it will be hard to succeed in real life. Yes, your teacher is there to help you and clear your doubts, but use their help only after doing everything you can and use it wisely. I don't mean that you should not ask them questions or clear doubts; of course, you should do those things, but at the same time, learn to work independently as well. Building wisdom and character must go hand in hand.

Our intelligence is not the same, and our strengths and weaknesses are different from each other. In your strength areas, you might not need to put in extra effort to be at the top, but it is important to give extra steps in your weak areas. Suppose your logical-mathematical intelligence is weak. In that case, this subject is your weak area, so you need to focus more energy and time on this subject.

Try to see the whole picture and not be narrow-minded when you fail. When I was studying in class 9, we had an exam the following week. One of my friends and I agreed to study together for the test. I went to their house on Friday evening and stayed until Sunday, the exam day.

On Friday night, we practised math until 2 AM; the next day, we studied from 6 AM until 1 AM. Even on Sunday, we had no break and used many practice papers. We were so confident in our efforts that we disorganized our practice papers on the floor, tables, and everywhere to impress their parents. We told ourselves that being a topper was not far from us and hoped to get the highest mark in math. We did our exam, and the results came out. To our surprise, my friend got 1 mark, and I got 3 marks out of 20 full marks, and we both failed.

Reflecting on our experience, studying just before the exam doesn't help much, making us more confused and destroying our grades. From that time onward, I started to study long before the exam and rest during the exam, allowing my mind to relax. I got higher marks and was free from exam stress.

From what I can understand from my experience, sudden preparation only destroys our confidence and embarrasses us. Studying should not be a project but a lifestyle, like eating food, where you study every day. Let's compare ourselves to the toppers. My friend and I studied intensively for two days and three nights, totalling 45 hours of practising maths. But the toppers have read for two hours every day since childhood. What would be the total hours they read until Class 9?

Please don't fool yourself as we did by studying only during exams and expecting good results. Studying is not a 100-meter race but a marathon. You must give a minimum of two hours daily to stay at the same level as your class. If you want to become an extraordinary student, study for five hours daily to stay ahead of your peers.

I will teach you how to read 5 times faster than your normal reading speed and memorize your notes in 50% less time than you are currently taking. These study tips and tools are scientifically proven, and many people have already used them. Genius World Record holders have used them for many years, and now they have become super brains. You can find all these study tips and tools in Chapter 4 of the study skill topic. However, to get the most out of this book, read it in sequence and don't jump to that page now.

In short, don't study just because you have an exam but because you love studying. You should be attracted to knowledge, not just school marks. Don't prepare for school exams only, but prepare yourself for life by studying your syllabus. Study continuously every day and rest during exams. Don't push yourself when the exam is near; studying at maximum during exams is bad for your health and mind. It will confuse you and put you under a lot of exam stress.

Entrepreneurial Habits and Mindset

This is something that we should teach every child in our families, and schools should take responsibility for educating them on this real-life matter as well. Saving is a skill, and if you have no skill in saving, you will waste your little money. Saving and investment must be taught at an early age.

Our society must function with an entrepreneurial mindset rather than relying on a government job attitude. In the Bible, God commanded his people to go into business and handle the economy even when they were in captivity by other nations. He didn't ask them to build his temple and pray to him while they were in other lands or kingdoms. He asked them to do business.

He who holds the economy or money has held power in every community. Do you want power? Learn about saving and investment. Jewish people are rich because they were taught how to save, invest, and do business from childhood. This is one of the reasons why Hitler hated them so much; they held the big business centre and controlled the German economy. They were outsiders to the German native speakers, but their economy and business were ruled by the Jews.

Our economy cannot grow because we depend on government and private jobs. The problem with jobs is that we don't produce products to export to other states. Jobs circulate money inside our community, but businesses can bring in money from other states and distribute it among the community, which increases our economic status. Another problem with jobs is that for one person to get richer, they must make someone else poorer in the community. But this is not the case in business; to get richer, you don't need to snatch money from your community; you can get it from other rich people from other states. This is the way to grow together as a community.

Yes, jobs are important, but if we only crave jobs and no one is willing to create employment opportunities through entrepreneurship and business, what will be our future? Many unemployed graduates are fighting for jobs, and those who are not good at studying won't find any. About 80% will be unemployed, and these people will be scared to get married, and a lot of single, unmarried men and women will rise, which will affect many things together.

Many of us think of business as evil, corrupted, and dishonest, but it doesn't have to be that way. Our parents and grandparents may not have had the education to run a truthful business, but we can do better in this generation. Excellent entrepreneur training is available that teaches how to conduct business with honesty and integrity. Most successful entrepreneurs have never lied; they live by sound principles. A poor-quality product needs to be supported by lies, but a high-quality product with a good strategy needs no lying to sell. In the long run, cheating, lying, and dishonesty always destroy businesses, so educated entrepreneur don't lie.

The Habit of Saving

"It's not about how much you earn; it's about how much you save."

Money is like a baby. If you invest in it and take good care of it, someday it will grow and take good care of you in times of sickness and emergency. Those who don't have savings don't have a secure future. How much do you have in your bank account if you suddenly get sick? Will it last three months? Can you feed yourself and your family for three months without working? An empty pocket is risky for our present and future lives. Every child needs to learn the art of saving to invest or protect themselves from disaster.

One good thing about having money in our pocket is that it boosts our self-esteem and builds confidence. I know this because I come from a poor family background. One time, while I was studying in class 12, my classmates organized an educational tour. I wanted to join but had no money, which my history teachers paid for me. I didn't even have money to buy my college uniform shoes. Ultimately, the discipline in charge had to give me his shoes to maintain college rules. Every student in high school could bring their Tiffin box for lunch whenever there were annual sports for a week. I know the feeling of not being able to afford one and acting like someone who is not hungry.

All these feelings create insecurities. I was nervous and panicked about continuing with my life, which is one reason I became depressed and attempted suicide twice during my class 10 studies.

While working as a warden at Lainat Ministry, I earned 8,000 per month. I bought a laptop and a soundbox, and the rest, I don't know how I spent my one-year salary. After I quit the job, I started running my own office and became broke. The first month, I didn't cook food. I didn't even have gas or a cooker to cook with. In the second month, I ate only once a day at a food hotel for a minimum cost of Rs.40 - only vegetables and rice.

After I published my first book, I received about 2 lakhs from it. About 60% was used for debt payment, and 35% for buying a certificate course. I carelessly wasted about Rs. 5,000 without keeping a record of it. After a few months, I became broke again."

Looking back at my experiences, I realize that I could have solved many of the problems and stresses I faced if I had the habit of saving. Our own bad habits are punishing us. If we don't consciously make an effort to create good habits, bad ones will automatically form in our lives. If I had reflected on and learned lessons from my life sooner, I would have become wiser and been able to avoid so many repeated mistakes and pain that I went through.

Not all of us are born with a silver spoon in our mouths. We must learn to earn, save, and invest from high school. If you are like me, learn to earn, save, and support instead of complaining about your life or your parents. They are many students disappointed in their parents for not being able to send them to good schools or colleges or for not giving them the birthday or Christmas gifts they desire. Those students must be taught how to earn, struggle, and learn what life actually is. Our parents did the best they could, and it's up to you to decide your future.

One good rule of parenting can be this: parents should provide what is necessary, and children should be given tasks and rewards that will be added to their savings, which the parents should keep aside for them. Children's desires should be bought from that amount. If you are a student and want to be successful, learn to take responsibility. Never ask your parents for your desires; ask them only for what you need, not what you want. Learn to earn and buy the things you want, starting with what you want, so that you don't have to depend on or trouble your parents for your needs when you grow up.

Learnt to Invest

While you are young, invest 80% of your time, energy, and money in personal development, such as learning, mastering new skills, and reading books. Invest 50% of your money in buying self-help books, starting from personal growth, mindset, motivational books, communication skills, leadership books, and so on. If you only spend time reading your school syllabus, you'll miss out on many relevant things for life.

Read your school syllabus for exams and career perspectives, and read other books about life-related matters. High school has no syllabuses to improve public speaking, communication, financial education, leadership skills, and so on. These things matter in life and will help you when you face challenges.

The school syllabus is not for life transformation; it is good for competitive exams and career matters. No one has said, "My school syllabus has opened up my mind, and from now on, I must become a better person." Don't be blinded by the school system and depend solely on the school syllabus for your life. 90% of graduates won't know about this. I learned the hard way during my depression, even having hallucinations and seeing things that were not real. Even after attempting suicide twice, the school syllabus didn't help.

From that time onward, my perspective on the school system completely changed. Please don't misunderstand me; I am not anti-school system. But it is time for students to learn to set boundaries with school and understand the reality and purpose of the school system. Academic learning is necessary for careers, competitive exams, national history, geography, famous world leaders, etc. For personal matters and issues, read other self-help books.

Just imagine if you read 30 minutes a day on any topic, such as a communication skills book. You'll master it in one year and stay ahead of your peers in one quality. We are all directly or indirectly competing with each other. If you compare or try to compete with your friend's beauty or dress, it will result in an inferiority complex. No matter how beautiful and handsome you are, you will still end up disappointed.

There is no certificate or someone to validate your ranking and confirm who is above or below in beauty. Everyone is unique and beautiful in their own way. I know this because I have a big scar on my nose, which makes me look ugly. However, I completely accept who I am and the way I am, and I never try to compete with others in terms of beauty. Instead, I secretly compete with my friends in knowledge and skills. Until I completed my graduation, I learned martial arts for 5 years and received a black belt certificate. I also joined NCC in high school, learned tailoring, learned computer skills, and received computer training 5 certificates, one of which is a DCA 1-year certificate.

Additionally, I received 15 public speaking training certificates, 20 fiction book writing certificates, and 19 more certificates in career counselling and related course. I earn people's respect simply because I keep learning and have skills that the majority do not possess. Due to that, I am much more confident than the most handsome person in the room, and my self-esteem is healthy.

I wanted to tell you this: compete with others in training, gain skills and certificates, read a lot of books, and increase your knowledge. Compete with your principal, not just your peers. This is a healthy way of competing with others, with many benefits. It keeps you diligent and makes you an expert. It also keeps you in shape, smarter, and up-to-date. And most of all, it keeps you ahead of your peers in your specific work area. Accept that you can't be above everyone else in everything, so choose your particular career, be the best in your field, and conquer others when it comes to your expertise.

To be an expert in any field:

1. Don't randomly read books.

2. Plan your reading.

3. Avoid fiction books that are read for fun and relaxation. Yes, you can read to broaden your perspective and vocabulary. Still, it's not worth investing time in fiction books when you can get the same perspective change and vocabulary improvement from non-fiction books.

One of the disadvantages of reading fiction books is that they shape your mood and character according to the book genre. If you read love story books, you'll most likely become involved in a relationship and take it seriously. One of my high school friends kept watching Korean, Thai, and Philippine romance movies and reading love stories. He always had relationship issues and was highly involved in relationships, and he finally got married at a young age before completing his graduation, as I predicted.

One of my classmates only read fiction love story books, and I kept advising her to start reading personal growth and self-help books. After three years of my suggestion, she finally read a self-help book and said, "It's so good to read self-help and personal growth books. I will focus on reading non-fiction books from now on." I am not totally against fiction books, but reading only fiction books does not provide much relevant information that can help us in our lives. Please read them, but the majority of your books should be non-fiction books. Reading fiction books are a waste of time.

In short, invest your time and money in buying and reading good books and learning new skills.

The Habit of Reading Books

Until 12th grade, I didn't have a proper plan and didn't read anything other than my academic syllabus. I had completed reading about 40 non-fiction books before finishing 12th grade. Only after that, I started planning and reading books properly to acquire a new set of skills. As an edupreneur, the way I read books is different from others. I read books to master a specific skill so that I can teach and give training in that field.

On the other hand, others read books so they might come in handy in the future. But as an edupreneur, I read 30 books in 3 months as much as possible. However, some school principals don't even read a single book monthly. Only a few people, about 20%, will read and complete one book in a year, excluding the academic syllabus and magazines. And only about 1% will have the habit of reading a book in our community. This is a sad truth.

Teachers must inspire their students to read by having the habit of reading books themselves. I have been given teacher training in many places, and I found out that the majority of teachers, about 80-90%, have not read a single book in 3 months. They only focus on their academic syllabus and teach what is inside their syllabus. Most graduates hardly open a book to read unless it is a competitive book for earning a job. This is where our school system has failed us; it has failed to cultivate the habit of reading books in students' lives.

We hate reading so much because we were never trained to read outside of our academic syllabus. Our parents don't read them, our teachers hardly read them, and few or none of our friends read them. And we became unaware of the benefits of reading books, especially self-help books.

Before I read "How to Win Friends and Influence People," I was not good at approaching and having conversations. I read and completed the book in one week, then tried out what was written inside. One early January morning, around 5:30 AM, I was on my way to college when I saw a big, tall man walking his big dog on the other side of the road. As we were going in the same direction, I approached him and started a conversation. The above book told said to talk to people based on their interests, not yours. So, I assumed that he was a dog lover, as he was walking his dog early in the morning during winter. I said, "Such a lovely dog, sir. What is your dog's name?" He replied with "XYZ" and continued to tell me how he got his dog and continue another 5 minutes. I stayed on the topic and commented on what I had read in the book.

As we continued the conversation, I said, "Dogs are intelligent animals. They can understand up to 250 words, and their nose prints are unique, like our fingerprints. They have no match with any other dog's nose print." He spoke for about 80% of the time just because I was talking to him about his interests, which is what the book suggested. After walking together for about 1 km, as we depart our way, he introduced himself as a physical doctor working inside the BSF camp near my house. As the book had suggested, I wrote down his name and details in my book.

He asked me, "If you need any medication, come and approach me anytime in the future. When you come to the gate, ask for me by name and say the house number. The duty army will call me, and I will let you in." I didn't give him any money, and we weren't relatives or had any common friends. But I gained his trust and favour just by talking to him about his interests, and I got his full name, address, and free medical check-up and medicine. This experience completely changed the way I viewed non-fiction books and the benefits of reading books. Before this experience, I had doubts that what was written in books wouldn't be practical or beneficial to our lives. But this experiment and experience gained my trust, and from there, I started reading self-help books.

Reading is a habit, and forming new habits is the toughest thing on earth. If forming habits were easy, most people would be rich and successful in life. Just because people are lazy in building new successful habits, they remain in their failure.

Now, I am going to share a life-changing habit. If you cultivate this habit, you will reap its rewards in folds of 100x. The investment is low and only takes a few hours, but the benefits will last forever in our lives. The book I read, "How to Win Friends and Influence People," during my 11th grade, has completely changed how I approach and talk to people. It solved many problems in my life, and even today, I use the principles written in that book.

Make a new commitment to form the habit of reading books. Every successful CEO reads 50 books per year, and the most successful ones at the top read 2-3 books per week. Your success highly depends on the number of books you read and the time you invest. I will tell you how to complete 50 books per year, whether you are a high school student or a working professional.

The average person reads 180-250 words per minute (WPM). Let's say you are a slow reader. Yes, every new reader is slow, and the speed comes with time. Now, let's assume that you read at a rate of 180 WPM, which is the slowest. An average book contains 35,000 words, and a short story will have 20,000 words or less. A novel will contain about 50,000 to 70,000 words on average. As I suggested, you should read self-help books, which every successful individual reads, and avoid fiction books. Let's assume your average book will be 30k to 40k words.

Suppose you read at the lowest speed of 180 words per minute as a new reader. If you read for only 15 minutes daily, you will read 2,700 words daily. In 13 days, you will complete one book containing 35,000 words, the average length for a self-help non-fiction book. In one month, you will read two books, and in one year, you will read 24 books as a new slow reader. If you read a single genre, say communication skills, after reading 24 books in that area, you will become an expert and know much more than anyone in your class or staff. This is achievable by spending only 15 minutes per day reading books.

But if you read for 30 minutes a day, you can complete 52 books in a year. By reading for 30 minutes, you can finish 5,400 words in a day. It will take only 7 days to complete one book, and in a single month, you'll be able to finish 4 books. On average, you can read over 50 books in a year. If you are a fast reader, you can complete more than 70 books with just 30 minutes of investment.

If you are not an edupreneur like me, you don't have to read hundreds of books on a single topic. That's why I encourage you to cultivate the habit of reading books. I advise you to pick the top 10 books each on leadership, communication, personal growth, mindset, finance, relationships, public speaking, parenting, and other beneficial topics relevant to our lives. Read the top 10 best books in each area, and repeat this every year by changing the subject. It can take your life to the next level, and the return can be 100 times more valuable than what you invest.

Cultivating the habit of reading a book is the fastest way to change your life. Reading provides exposure to fresh ideas, granting new perspectives that can profoundly alter your entire existence. While a single book may not make a significant impact, immersing yourself in the subject matter of thirty books certainly will. As you continue to read, your mindset and cognitive framework undergo transformation. By repeatedly focusing on a particular subject, it becomes more prominent in your mind, leading to conscious and subconscious mental engagement with that topic. Engaging in the habit of reading not only enhances your knowledge but also positively transforms your mind and character, providing a chance to achieve success. My personal experience corroborates this; when I faced depression in 2015, medication failed to cure me, but reading books played a significant role in my recovery.

Time Management

Those who manage their time well are the most productive and have a fulfilled life. They have time for fun, work, and helping others. But those who lack time management have no time for themselves or others.

Have you ever wondered why everyone has the same amount of time, i.e., 24 hours each day, whether rich or poor, yet at the end of the day, our results and productivity are not the same? Some people wisely invest their time and use it consciously to earn lakhs, while others waste their time and cause trouble without earning.

How we spend our time determines the value of our time, and we are defined by how we spend our time. If we always go to a bar and drink alcohol, we'll be called an alcoholic, and if we always read books, we'll be called a bookworm. The way we spend our time defines our quality of life. To improve the quality of our lives, we must spend more of our time doing quality and valuable things.

A great and successful person is simply someone whose time is valuable because they make it a habit to attend only worthy and valuable events. If you try to see your neighbour, a common person, you can see him immediately in the morning or at night, but if you try to see your Chief Minister, you may have to wait a week to get the opportunity. What about the president or prime minister? You may seek the opportunity to see them for a month, but there is a high chance that you won't succeed. All successful people focus on using their time for only valuable and beneficial things, while all poor and unsuccessful people don't spend their time consciously, focusing on spending their time wisely. If you want to be valuable, start using your time for valuable things.

The term "time management" is incorrect. It should be "people management." In reality, it's about managing and disciplining ourselves. No matter how you manage it, you can't shorten or lengthen your 24 hours. But if you manage yourself well, you can be 10 times more productive than not managing yourself.

The quality of your time does not depend on how many hours you have left. It depends on how wisely you use them and how many quality things you do. If Gandhi were still alive today, world peace would be much stronger. His time on earth would be more valuable than a serial killer living for 100 years. We can't guarantee that we will live for 60 years or die as old men, but we can ensure that we will live each day doing valuable things and be remembered even after death for 100 years.

Our lives and time cannot be separated; they are two sides of the same coin. When you waste your time, you waste your life and vice versa. If you love your life, try to spend your time carefully and do beneficial things for yourself. If you can't do helpful things for yourself, do them for others. Your hands can always be a blessing to others; help your family or community members. Your mouth can be a blessing to others; speak good words and start praising others. Your ears can be a blessing to others; listen to others' problems attentively when they share, and they will feel relaxed, understood, and loved. Being a blessing or a curse is just a few steps away from us.

Here are a few steps on how to manage yourself for maximum productivity. If you are lazy, you don't need time management; you won't do things even if you plan your day. The way to save time is **Vision + Plan + Action = Productivity**, which saves our time. Just before you go to sleep, close your eyes and visualize tomorrow. Ask yourself, "What are the things I need to complete tomorrow?" "What is my top priority for tomorrow that cannot be delayed?" "What can I delegate to others to do for me?"

Time Management

Here is how to prioritize your day

- List the top 3 most important tasks that you should complete no matter what.
- List the tasks that can be delayed and done the next day, but if you have time, it's better to complete them today.
- List 3 fun activities, such as watching a movie, going to the park, or calling a friend, and don't set a specific time for them. Instead, make time for them as a reward after completing your top-priority tasks. But never start with the fun activities, no matter how tempting they seem. Some people keep the fun activities for later if they still have time after completing everything, which is not motivating and an unproductive way to use your time.

Start your day by doing the most difficult task. Once you finish it, you'll feel productive and be more motivated to complete the less difficult tasks. Please don't save the most difficult task for last, as you may not have the energy or enough time to complete it. There is a big chance that you will procrastinate the next day. Put the difficult task first; it will only destroy motivation and self-esteem if you don't complete your daily to-do list.

Some people may say that if they start with the easiest task, completing them will motivate them to do more. This is not true.

You may complete the easiest task, but there is no self-worth as it is not a difficult thing to do. While you have energy, time, and full attention, do the most challenging task. But remember to prioritize and do more of what is working. Don't just do the difficult task, as it may be the least productive. But if it is among your priorities, do it first.

Learn to double up on whatever works in your life that adds value. Authors spend more time writing than on any other task. If you write more, you'll earn more, gain more respect, and help more people, doubling everything. So, write more. For students spend more time reading and studying than on any other task. If you study more, you'll get better grades, gain respect from peers, and receive appreciation from teachers and parents.

While talking about being diligent and hardworking, you don't have to be diligent and hardworking in everything. You are a human being who has limited time, energy, and attention. But you must, by all means, be diligent and hardworking, and be willing to do anything related to your career and success. Learn to prioritize your tasks; this can improve everything in your life.

You can't be in two places simultaneously, so choose the most productive place for yourself. You can't be diligent at everything, so learn to determine where you'll spend your energy and time. You can't afford to make mistakes in prioritizing your tasks. People will keep telling you their priorities and try to persuade you to do something other than what you need to do. But stay firm and stand your ground.

Choose wisely what you will spend 70% of your waking hours and what else you need to do to achieve that goal. List all the things that can help you achieve your goal faster, and start doing what you can, even if you are still a student. For example, suppose you are a student studying in eighth grade and want to become a doctor. In that case, you should know which subjects you need to be good at, such as physics, biology, and chemistry, especially biology. Let's say English is a compulsory subject and is necessary for any career. Make sure you pass every subject and try to score the highest mark on those subjects that are specifically needed in your career. Besides that, try to find out the right mindset and habits for doctors and cultivate them.

2. Timebank; Invest all your minutes and second

Who wills you respect more, someone with Rs.10 Crores or Rs. 10 rupees in his bank account? Your trust, respect, and admiration will go to the person with more money in his bank. This is exactly what happens to us when we don't have much money in our bank, right?

Imagine there is a bank that only stores up the valuable time you spend on every second of your life. If you study for 2 hours today and spend the rest of your time doing nothing useful, only 2 hours will be stored in your time bank. The lost time cannot be replaced or recouped, and you cannot store it for one month. It would be best if you stored every second and minute, or it would be wasted and forever gone.

Now, how much precious time do you have in your time bank? Will your total valuable time be 1,000 hours or 100 hours? Or will it be zero because you are lazy and have never done anything great? Or will your real valuable time spend 1,000 hours out of your current age?

How many hours have you spent doing something beneficial and valuable every day? When our total valuable time spent is less, our quality and productivity become limited, and our source of income decreases. With less valuable time spent, we have time for criticizing, complaining, and doing bad things.

If you hear criticism about yourself, you are walking too slowly and not far away from the critics. Walk fast, do a lot of things, and have many daily goals and tasks. Don't have time for doing evil things or getting angry over small things. Don't walk behind others and envy them. Don't walk slowly and hear their criticism. Walk fast and achieve personal goals while they sit idle with no purpose.

3. Proper daily routine

Let's go back to when our ancestors lived in villages and cultivated fields. They were mentally and physically stronger and healthier than us. They did not suffer from stress and anxiety the way we do today. They never lacked sleep and had a good appetite. They didn't need a gym; they walked 3 or more kilometres daily and worked from early morning till evening. There were none or few lazy people who sat idle.

Our modern lifestyle has destroyed our mental and physical health, as well as our spiritual life and ethics. Most of us now don't sleep as we're told not to sleep before midnight. We wake up late and never get the chance to see the sunrise, which can affect our mood for the day. We don't have a proper structure and routine for our daily lives, especially for adults living in cities and towns.

The universe, our Milky Way, the sun, and plants, the way they evolve and rotate, is structured and organized; we can trust it because of this. We can rely on someone with a structured and organized lifestyle to use it beneficially. If you are the CEO of a company, and your staff do not have a proper and organized lifestyle, the company won't be effective and productive. To be resourceful and productive, we need to have a healthy lifestyle suitable for our work and environment. We're not as fresh as a person who wakes up early, and early energy can be used productively. I'm not saying that waking up early is good, and you must wake up early by any means. If you have night work, it is impossible. But for students, we can sleep early and wake up early. There is no need to sleep late, wake up early, and not have enough sleep. Sleeping late and waking up late are also not good for our health.

Are you living like an addicted person? An addicted person no longer has proper time for food, sleep, and structure in their daily life. If you are a gamer or addicted to computer or mobile games, it still applies to you. Or if you're addicted to anything, it will affect your timing, and you won't maintain a proper daily routine. If you wake up at 6 AM and have breakfast at 7 AM, try to maintain that routine. Don't keep changing your breakfast, lunch, and dinner timings, as it's bad for your digestive system and can affect your health.

CHAPTER THREE

BEYOND THE CLASSROOM: HOW TO NAVIGATE CAREER CHOICES AND FIND YOUR CALLING WITH A MENTOR AND OUTSIDE PERSPECTIVE

Have you ever wondered how our great-grandfathers educated themselves and earned a livelihood before the school education system? Of course, they had intelligence, and some were educated, though not to the same extent as in our time. They did not have medical training but knew about medicinal plants and how to give birth. In fact, some women gave birth alone in small tents. There were no classrooms, theory classes, or practical classes like today.

Some people may say they were uncivilized and that we are much better than them. However, we still have so many lessons to learn from them.

Career before the School System

Have you ever wondered how people acquired knowledge and skills before the school system? Parents teach their children a way of life, ethics, and societal norms. Grandparents helped educate their grandsons. No classroom was needed. Every night before sleep was story time and history class. They learned everything while doing practical work and then theory. They were more industrious than us. They couldn't wait to learn through theory and just did things even without guidance. They were confident and bold compared to the new generation, many of whom were afraid to start a new adventure. They made many mistakes, and that's how they learned a better way. Now, we don't allow our children or students to make mistakes. We scold and embarrass them in school, which injects fear and makes them avoid trying new things. In one way, they have fewer mistakes but fail to learn many lessons.

They worked closely with their teachers, staying in the same house, eating at the same table, and facing everything together. Yes, I am talking about the relationship between father and son or mother and daughter. A father and son may go hunting together, and the child learns from his father, who received an education from his father and has more than 20 years of experience. The child is physically present in the field with an expert, not in a classroom with only theories.

Modern education may give us information, but it excludes the hardship, experience, and required skills for children. Some adults can't make their own decisions, avoid responsibilities, and can't be used effectively in any field because they lack the necessary character and skills. They may have knowledge but not the character or skills needed to survive in life. This may be one reason so many graduates can still not take care of themselves.

Family occupations flow down from father to son and from generation to generation. However, in this 21st century, most jobs will keep changing, and what you wish to become while young can disappear when you become an adult. Jobs disappear faster, and new jobs arise so quickly. In just ten years, helicopter pilots, cameramen, and reporters lost their jobs because drones replaced them. Bus drivers were replaced by AI-driven autonomous vehicles. According to experts, lawyers and doctors will also be replaced in the future with AI and mobile apps. So, if you are going for doctors and lawyers, try to be a specialist in your field, and you won't be able to replace with AI or a phone app. Instead of selecting the position you want to work in, choose the domain you want to work in, learn everything, and acquire all the skills needed to succeed in that domain. This will be the safest way. What's safe is no longer secure, and the new generation needs to have the vision to choose a career.

Wrong Perspective

One common misconception that many of us still hold is that school guarantees us a job. While this may be true for a few, it is not true for many. If it were true, we wouldn't have so many unemployed graduates. Before the 1980s, when our fathers or grandfathers finished their 10th grade, the whole village would celebrate by killing a cow or pig. But now, even if you finish your degree, no one celebrates with you except your family. Why is that? Because there are so many graduates now, we no longer feel it's worth celebrating. In our fathers' or grandfathers' time, only a few could clear the 10th-grade exam, which was considered precious and celebrated as if he had cleared the Civil Service Examination.

In our grandfathers' time, once they graduated, jobs chased them, and some unwillingly ended up in high-ranking positions. The reason was simple - so few graduates and many jobs needed to be filled. Now, it's the opposite - many graduates, but very few jobs are available. Despite this, many parents and grandparents still believe that once their child gets an education, they will automatically get a job once they graduate.

It is estimated that only about 10% of students in a classroom are naturally good at studies. The rest need hard work from teachers, parents, and the students themselves. Not all students are born with the same level of intelligence, and not all students in the same class have equal level of "logical-mathematical intelligence," yet parents and teachers try their best to make those students good at mathematics.

In this modern world, we need to be careful with our expectations for our children, as it can be a huge burden for the child if they do not have the intelligence or personality for a certain job. Parents need help from career counsellors to find their child's inborn qualities, intelligence, and personality or to see which job is suitable for their children. Career counsellors need to conduct DMIT, psychometric, and personality tests to determine what is best for the child. We'll talk more about this in the next chapter.

From age 11 to age 19, A Mentor

Before the school system was established, when a child reached the age of 12, they were asked which profession they wanted to pursue, such as blacksmithing, book writing, farming, etc. The child would then choose one, and if they wished to become a blacksmith, their family would find them the best blacksmith in their town or city. The child would stay with the blacksmith, working for them and doing anything they asked including the house chores, not just the work. If the child wanted to become a writer, their family would find them the best author in town or city, and the child would stay with them, working as their assistant. The child would receive no pay or salary but would work closely with their mentor for about 8 years, from 12 to 20 age. During this time, the child would gain all the knowledge, attitudes, characteristics, and skills necessary for their profession. They would know their mentor inside out, just as their mentor would know them.

After 8 years, when the child reached the age of 20, they had the freedom to set up their own business and start earning for themselves. While the child was flexible and on a high learning stage, they were taught their profession and specific skill. This ensured that the child would be efficient in their work. The school system doesn't do this. Until 16, a child is in high school, still uncertain about what they want to do in life. At around the age of 22, they graduate, and some continue their studies further. During all their flexible and learning years, they spend their time in school learning theories. After graduation, they begin to look for jobs and acquire the necessary skills. If the child is good in studies, they will definitely clear competitive exams, but if not, there is a high chance that they will not clear the exam even after 5 years. Only about 10% of graduates secure government jobs, while the rest work in the private sector or start their own businesses.

To work in the private sector or independently, one needs skills. In private companies, experience and skill set are more important than academic performance. Even if someone gets a first-class degree, they can be fired if they can't generate income for the company. Conversely, someone who earns a third-class degree but can bring massive income and growth to the company with their skills will see their promotion come quickly and their income double within a few years. In private businesses, academic performance is not as important as skill, character, or attitude.

In short, parents trust schools to provide jobs for their children, but schools focus on passing percentages and marks rather than on preparing students' character and skills for their careers. 90% of parents' expectations are failing due to the school system's failure to change its approach to education and lack emphasize on practical skills. Approximately 90% of students won't excel in their studies, so it's crucial to emphasize improving their abilities and character instead of just their grades.

There is life outside of the school building as well. There is a life of luxury even outside of academic institutions. Many of us think that school is the only way to succeed in life or the only option for living a luxurious life. We aim for a government job, and if someone can't get a government job, we assume they have an uncertain future. But is this the reality? Of course not. Many entrepreneurs and wealthy business owners have not graduated, and 59% are self-made billionaires. If your son or daughter is not good at studies, don't push them. Instead, make a plan for their future that does not involve competitive examinations.

We mistakenly think that all graduates are educated and that all those who don't finish a degree are uneducated. We only consider someone educated if they can use their knowledge for a profession and support their family. You may be a graduate, but if you can't use your head to support your family, you may not be educated person. The terms educated and academic success are not the same. Instead of focusing on marks and percentages, why not focus on a career? Don't study just for passing marks; it's not worth it. You can clear your degree in the first class but still be an unemployed graduate. Focus on your calling, your passion, and your career. These should be your reasons for studying, and you should not quit school when you fail exam or lose motivation. Academics are there to help us only; it's not our main goal.

You can't say academics are unimportant and mention that even Steve Jobs didn't graduate. Their situation and ours are not the same. Let me explain to you. If you were born in America, you wouldn't need to learn the world language, i.e. English, as it's your native language. You can read, write and use English everywhere, even in most countries. Secondly, America is the land of opportunities; they have business connections with every nation, and you don't have to learn much about other languages as everyone or most people have learnt English. Thirdly, you'll be able to use your currency anywhere, and the US dollar is more valuable than most other currencies. Starting and doing business will be much smoother than anywhere else. Of many reasons, these three are the most important ones.

Now, if you were born in another country than the US, you must go to school to learn English. Where else will you learn grammar and writing than school? Everything or the most important information is written in English, not your language. All the important books are written in English, including leadership, personal growth, communication, and parenting. If you cut yourself off from English, you lose the opportunity to access many relevant pieces of information. Whether you're going to be a footballer, cricketer, businessman, or any other line of work, study at least until class 12 to learn English without any problems. If you're lazy or weak in your studies, study till 12. But read as much as possible if you study for English learning purposes.

Don't just stay inside the classroom and do nothing. Go out, do different things, and learn as many skills as possible that are relevant to your career. This way, you'll survive. If you're not good at studies and still do nothing except go to school, you'll become an unemployed graduate, and it won't be easy to find a job, even in the private sector, without skills. Parents and teachers must be aware of this and lead their children to a better profession or career suitable for the child."

Be aware of the School system

The school system and army rules are similar. They are both trained for a specific purpose. The only difference is that the army selects the fittest among many candidates, while students are all chosen to follow the school education system, despite their uniqueness.

These days, some schools are selecting only the best students, forgetting why schools were created in the first place - to train the gifted and excellent students only? The purpose of schools should be to train the worst into the best possible version of a student. The rich and excellent in studies attend better schools, but have we checked how many students got employment and have a successful life after 5 years?

Schools should compete not on percentages and marks but on building real-life successful students, not just on studies but also in other areas of life. The scale on which schools should compete and how parents should select the best school for their child should be based on how many students got jobs in the government and private sectors or started their own businesses.

We must be willing to be unique and keep our unique perspective, no matter what. The longer we stay in academics, the more we believe that to create something new, we must learn till PhD first and study everything others have done. The more we stay in academia, the less we want to be unique, as everyone wants to be accepted.

Our creativity and original ideas are slowly shut down as they are awkward among others. We get slapped with words of criticism, not because our works and ideas are bad, but because they are unique. Our craving to start something new has gone the longer we stay in academia, as we are being intelligently questioned and mocked, "This is not the way, it has never happened in this way, this is not supported by this, it's impossible no one has ever done this, first finish your studies." These are discouraging words we hear in school that decrease our confidence, creativity, and uniqueness. While the school has taught us many good lessons, we should never allow the school to instil fear in us.

School systems are created so that the government can empower and control us. There is nothing wrong with that, and we should obey the rules of our land. But be very careful not to be brainwashed by the school system to let you think that to make a livelihood, school is the only way. There are lives outside of school. But a job is super required if you want to work as an employee for the rest of your life. However, a job is not the only means of livelihood. You can always start your own office, business, or farming. And if you really do a good job in business, you'll be richer and freer than those who have a job in the government or private sector. You'll have staff and employees who are graduates and good at studies working under you. So, don't lose hope, even if your percentage is bad. We shall discuss this more in the next chapter.

CHAPTER FOUR

Choosing Your Path: A Guide to Career Selection, Self-Worth, and Goal Setting for a Purposeful Life

Why is a career so important in our life?

First, careers can provide a means of financial security. A steady income can allow a man to provide for himself and his family, pay bills, save for the future, and live a comfortable lifestyle. This financial stability can bring peace of mind and reduce stress, leading to a higher quality of life.

Second, careers can be a source of personal fulfilment. Pursuing one's interests, developing skills, and making a positive impact in a chosen field can give a sense of purpose and achievement. As men work towards their career goals, they can develop a sense of mastery and expertise that can boost confidence and self-esteem. Furthermore, as men gain experience and progress in their careers, they may also have the opportunity to take on more challenging and rewarding roles.

Third, careers can contribute to a man's identity and status. A person's job often plays a significant role in their social identity and status. For example, being a doctor or lawyer can carry a certain prestige and respect in society, and some men may find that the status they gain from their careers is important to them. Additionally, a career can reflect a person's values and ambitions and be a way for men to express themselves and their unique talents and interests.

Fourth, careers can provide opportunities for social connections. Working in a particular field can expose men to a diverse range of people with similar interests and goals. These connections can lead to opportunities for collaboration, mentorship, and networking. Furthermore, positive relationships with co-workers can contribute to job satisfaction and happiness.

Fifth, careers can be a way for men to make a positive contribution to society. Many careers involve working to help others, such as in healthcare, education, or social work. Other careers include advancing scientific knowledge or creating new products and services that benefit society. Contributing to the community in a meaningful way can give men a sense of purpose and fulfilment that goes beyond personal gain.

Overall, careers can be a significant aspect of a man's life, providing financial security, personal fulfilment, a sense of identity and status, social connections, and opportunities to contribute to society. While not all men may prioritize their careers, it can be an essential part of their lives for many.

Many of us choose a life partner more carefully than our career. Our purpose in life is to work while we can, and marriage is not compulsory for many of us. You can live without getting married, but not without a job. How will you afford food, clothing, medicine, shelter, etc., if you don't earn anything? I do not mean marriage is bad, but it a secondary to our lives. From early childhood, we focus on our careers and spend 18-20 years in studies to get a better job. And 2/3 of our day time is spent working unless you are a lazy man who does nothing. The average office hours are from 9AM to 4PM, and some will continue to work even at night. The shocking news is that 90% of people never ever consider and spend months and years considering which career they should choose.

45% of Students make the wrong career choice, and 70% of employees are dissatisfied with their current job. A staggering 93% of students 14-21 are aware of just seven career options out of 250-300 job opportunities in India.

- India Today Survey Report

I had gone to many schools and colleges for career guidance seminars and had given over 300 workshops and training at different places. In all the schools I have been to, I asked students how many had a clear idea about their aim in life, what they want to become when they grow up, and what career you are going for. Most young students have aim in life, but the more class they study, the lesser they have dreams.

Whenever I ask class 9 and 10 students to raise their hands if they have a dream or aim in life. About 25% raise their hand and about 15% for classes eleven and twelve. This means that many of them give up their dream due to financial issues or lack of knowledge about their life goals. And many students have never had an aim in life. Parents and teachers can't help them as they are not career counsellors. Parents and teachers can show different career options but don't know the student career matching.

There are many career options in India, and about 250-300 career choices can be made by single students. And one has to know their matching career before one can choose their path. Many students are anxious about their careers and afraid they might choose the wrong one. One of my clients is doing her degree and wants to be IAS, already starting her preparation for Civil Service Examination. After some months, she couldn't prepare again with many doubts and finally met me. After doing Psychometric Career

Aptitude Test, she got 87%, matching her dream, which is also the highest recommendation for her based on her career test. And this is what she wrote to me;

For ages and ages, I have been trying to break through the barriers of doubt about my career choice. The lingering questions know no bounds, like, what if I'm not a good match for this career? Will I be capable enough? Am I actually confident that it's right for me? So on and so forth; the worst of all-WILL, THIS CAREER BE A SUCCESS TO ME?

But there is something grand about the career counselling session with Mr Sang that works miracles for me. Now, I know he's an excellent career coach. The psychometric test he provides is a life-changer that quenches all my thirst for career struggle. He has been pivotal in helping me better understand the reality of my career choice. Not only did he interpret the test results, but dig deep down into the huge scope of the career I opted for. Undeniably, he clarified all my accumulated doubts, so I broke free from my uncertainties. I am truly grateful to him beyond words.

-by Jemima Ngaihdim, Dorcus veng

As a career counsellor, we first conduct the DMIT Lifetime test and Psychometric Career Aptitude test on the student to know their inborn and current abilities, intelligence, personality, learning style, career recommendation, interest, skill set and career recommendation. We also give the student some homework to help them realize their passion. And we ask several questions and see all the test reports and student home assignments to find out their passion, also their parent's desired career for their Child. And we don't choose a career for the student; we only show the matching career they have and what their parents wish for them, and we help them make the right decision.

Yes, of course, we encourage the student to take their career decision only to those career matches they had. Once they decide, we build career paths and plan to achieve them. We help the student with whatever issues they have in their studies, slow memory and poor subjects. We help them improve those problems by teaching those learning techniques and study skills.

If they want to discontinue, their academic studies or their families can't support them. We help them get scholarships and admission under TIS or government-funded colleges. But still, if you want to quick their studies, we can't force the student to continue. For that, we give different options such as certification courses and diploma courses so that they can continue their career without completing their graduation. If they study till class 10, we should show their career path, certification course and diploma course after class 10 or class 12 if they had done till 12.

If the students are looking for new admission in other states or countries, we also help them find suitable colleges and the admission process. If they are seeking admission abroad, we give information about the countries' conditions, fee structures, visa details, and whether they are friendly countries. We can provide them based on their needs; we have a list of more than 200 top colleges in India and the world. If you want to study further for any stream, paramedical lines, certification course and diploma course.

If my clients are graduates seeking a job, as a career counsellor, we help them find suitable careers. We help them with CV or Resume writing and job details and teach them interview skills if needed. Psychometric Career Aptitude test, Job Fitment Test and DMIT Lifetime are the three tests that I conducted on them to know their matching career.

Mostly career counselling has 3 sessions and completes within one month. Career counselling or coaching sessions are based on the students' needs. Career counselling focuses more on the student's emotional issues and decision-making, while career coaching focuses more on the future and goal development of the student's career. That is why we provide both services.

What is career matching, and why is it needed?

Career matching is the process of matching an individual's unique characteristics, such as their skills, interests, personality, values, and aspirations, with a suitable career path or occupation. The goal is to identify a career that is a good fit for the individual in terms of personal fulfilment and professional success.

The need for career matching arises from the fact that many people are not sure what career path they should pursue, or they may not have a clear understanding of the types of careers that are a good fit for their skills and personality. For example, a person may be good at math and science but may not necessarily want to pursue a career in engineering or medicine. Conversely, another person may have a strong interest in music and art but may not be aware of the various career paths in these fields.

Without career matching, individuals may find themselves in careers that do not suit their strengths or interests, leading to a lack of fulfilment and job dissatisfaction. This can result in individuals feeling unfulfilled or unhappy in their jobs and potentially even switching careers multiple times in their lifetime.

To avoid the above, career matching is required that involves:

- Assessing the individual's unique characteristics can be done through various methods, such as career assessments or psychometric career aptitude test.
- Job matching software or candidate aptitude test.
- Working with a career counsellor or coach.

These tools help individuals identify their skills, personality traits, values, and interests and match them with potential career paths or occupations.

Career matching can also help people make more informed decisions when choosing a college major, pursuing additional education or training, or considering a career change. By identifying careers that are a good fit for their unique characteristics, individuals can choose a career path more likely to lead to personal and professional fulfilment.

Ultimately, career matching can help individuals find a career that aligns with their values and allows them to achieve their personal and professional goals. It is an important tool for anyone seeking to find their calling and wants to make the most of their skills and potential.

In short; if you have a career matching your work, you'll be happy and satisfied which will motivate you to work harder eventually this will improve your performance and increase your productivity. And you will be promoted faster and earn more than someone who works isn't matching, who hates his job and is unmotivated for work.

What is career maturity, and why is it important for students?

Career maturity refers to an individual's level of readiness and preparation for making effective and informed career decisions. It involves a combination of cognitive, emotional, and behavioural factors, such as self-awareness, self-confidence, decision-making skills, knowledge of the job market and various career paths.

Career maturity is particularly important for students as they approach the transition from school to the world of work. This can be a challenging time for many students as they are faced with important decisions about their future careers and may lack the experience and knowledge necessary to make informed choices.

Having a high level of career maturity can help students make more informed decisions about their future career paths. It can also help them feel more confident and prepared as they enter the job market, leading to greater success and job satisfaction.

Here are some specific ways in which career maturity can benefit students:

1. **Self-awareness:** Career maturity involves a deep understanding of one's own interests, values, and strengths. By developing this self-awareness, students can identify career paths that align with

their personal characteristics, leading to greater job satisfaction and career success.

2. **Decision-making skills:** Career maturity also involves the ability to make effective decisions. By developing decision-making skills, students can weigh the pros and cons of different career paths and choose the best suited to their interests, abilities, and goals.

3. **Networking:** Career maturity involves building relationships and networking with professionals in one's desired career field. This can help students learn more about the job market and various career paths and make connections that may lead to job opportunities in the future.

4. **Job readiness:** Career maturity involves developing the skills and knowledge necessary to succeed in one's chosen career path. By developing these skills and gaining relevant experience, students can increase their job readiness and become more competitive in the job market.

In short, career maturity is important for students because it helps them make more informed decisions about their future careers, feel more confident and prepared as they enter the job market, and ultimately achieve greater success and job satisfaction.

Why is a career important to a person?

Choosing a career is important for several reasons, including:

1. **Personal fulfilment**

A fulfilling career can provide a sense of purpose and meaning, leading to greater happiness and well-being. When we enjoy our work and feel meaningful, we are more likely to be motivated and satisfied with our lives.

Absolutely, personal fulfilment is a crucial aspect of choosing a career. When we find work that aligns with our interests, values, and strengths, we are more likely to experience a sense of purpose and meaning in our lives. This can contribute to greater happiness, satisfaction, and overall well-being.

Finding a career that provides personal fulfilment can also increase motivation and engagement in the workplace. When we enjoy what we do, we are more likely to put in the effort to excel and contribute in meaningful ways. This can lead to career success and professional growth over time.

It's important to note that personal fulfillment can take many different forms. For some people, it may involve pursuing a career that aligns with their passions or allows them to make a positive impact in the world. For others, it may involve finding work that provides a healthy work-life balance or enables them to spend time with loved ones. Ultimately, the key is finding a career that aligns with one's values, interests, and goals and provides a sense of purpose and meaning.

Of course, finding a fulfilling career is not always easy. It can require a lot of self-reflection, research, and exploration. It may also involve taking risks, making sacrifices, and adapting to changing circumstances. However, for many, the effort is worth it, as a fulfilling career can provide a foundation for a happy and meaningful life.

2. Financial stability

A career can provide financial stability and security, allowing us to support ourselves and our families. A career can provide a steady income that allows us to support ourselves and our families and plan for the future. A good career can lead to a comfortable standard of living, including the ability to save for the future and provide for our loved ones. Yes, financial stability is an important reason why choosing a career is important.

Financial stability can lead to a comfortable standard of living, including having a safe home, access to quality healthcare and education, and the ability to enjoy leisure activities and travel. A good career can also allow us to save for the future, whether it be for retirement, emergencies, or other goals.

When we have the resources to meet our basic needs and plan for the future, we can focus on other aspects of our lives, such as personal growth, relationships, and hobbies. Moreover, financial stability can also reduce stress and worry, which can have a positive impact on our overall well-being. It's important to note that financial stability can mean different things to different people. Some may prioritize a high income or a prestigious job title, while others may prioritize work-life balance or flexibility. The key is to find a career that provides a level of financial stability that aligns with one's goals and priorities.

Overall, financial stability is a critical aspect of choosing a career. It can provide the resources and security necessary to support oneself and loved ones and allow for the pursuit of personal and professional goals.

3. Professional development

Choosing a career allows us to develop our skills and knowledge in a particular area, leading to personal and professional growth. Investing in our careers allows us to become experts in our field and continue to learn and grow over time. Yes, professional development is another important reason why choosing a career is important. A career can provide the opportunity to develop new skills, gain knowledge, and become an expert in a particular field. This ongoing development can lead to personal and professional growth over time.

Professional development can take many forms, depending on the industry and the individual's goals and interests. It can involve taking courses or training programs, attending conferences and workshops, seeking mentors or networking opportunities, and working on challenging projects or assignments.

Investing in professional development can lead to various benefits, including increased job satisfaction, better job performance, and increased career advancement opportunities. It can also lead to greater flexibility and adaptability as individuals become more skilled and knowledgeable in their field.

Moreover, professional development can provide a sense of fulfillment and purpose, as individuals can see their progress and growth over time. It can also lead to a sense of pride and accomplishment as individuals become recognized as experts in their field.

Overall, professional development is an essential aspect of choosing a career. By investing in one's skills and knowledge, individuals can continue learning and growing, leading to greater personal and professional fulfillment.

4. Contribution to society

Many careers provide opportunities to make a positive impact on society, whether through providing services, creating products, or solving problems. By choosing a career that aligns with our values and interests, we can make a difference in the world and contribute to the greater good. Absolutely, contribution to society is another important reason why choosing a career is important. Many careers provide opportunities to make a positive impact on society, whether through providing services, creating products, or solving problems. By choosing a career that aligns with our values and interests, we can make a difference in the world and contribute to the greater good.

Contributing to society can take many forms, depending on the individual's interests and the industry. A career in science or technology can lead to new discoveries or innovations that benefit society, while a career in social work can help vulnerable populations get the support they need. For example, a healthcare career can provide the opportunity to help people recover from illness or injury, while a career in education can help children develop the skills and knowledge they need to succeed in life.

Moreover, contributing to society can provide a sense of purpose and fulfillment beyond financial gain or personal success. By making a difference in the lives of others, individuals can feel that they are contributing to something larger than themselves and that their work has meaning and value.

It's important to note that not all careers provide the same level of opportunity to make a positive impact on society. However, even in industries that may not have an obvious societal impact, individuals can still find ways to contribute to their communities and make a difference in the world.

Overall, contribution to society is a critical aspect of choosing a career. By aligning one's interests and values with a career that provides opportunities to make a positive impact, individuals can find greater fulfillment and purpose in their work and contribute to the greater good.

5. Life-long learning

A career can provide continuous learning and growth opportunities. As technologies and industries evolve, there is always something new to learn, which can keep our minds sharp and engaged over time. As technologies and industries evolve, there is always something new to learn, and staying up-to-date can lead to personal and professional growth. Yes, life-long learning is another important reason why choosing a career is important. A career can provide continuous learning and growth opportunities, which can keep our minds sharp and engaged over time.

Life-long learning can take many forms, depending on the industry and the individual's goals and interests. It can involve taking courses or training programs, attending conferences and workshops, seeking mentors or networking opportunities, and working on challenging projects or assignments.

Investing in life-long learning can lead to various benefits, including increased job satisfaction, better job performance, and increased career advancement opportunities. It can also lead to greater flexibility and adaptability as individuals become more skilled and knowledgeable in their field.

Moreover, life-long learning can provide a sense of fulfilment and purpose, as individuals can grow and improve over time. It can also lead to a sense of pride and accomplishment as individuals become recognized for their expertise and contributions.

Overall, life-long learning is a critical aspect of choosing a career. By investing in one's skills and knowledge over time, individuals can continue to learn and grow, leading to greater personal and professional fulfilment. This can also help individuals stay engaged and motivated throughout their careers.

In short, choosing a career is important for personal fulfilment, financial stability, professional development, contribution to society, and life-long learning. By taking the time to identify and pursue a career that aligns with our values, interests, and goals, we can create a meaningful and rewarding life for ourselves.

The wrong way most people select their career

Most people prioritize their career choices based on factors like income, demand, stream selection, aptitude, personality, and interest. However, this approach can be flawed and lead to dissatisfaction and unfulfillment in one's career. Prioritizing income and demand may seem like practical considerations, but they can result in pursuing a career solely for financial gain rather than personal fulfillment. Choosing a career based solely on stream selection, without considering one's aptitude or interest, can lead to struggling in a job that doesn't align with one's skills or passions.

Additionally, prioritizing personality over interest can result in settling for a career that fits one's personality but doesn't necessarily bring satisfaction or a sense of purpose. Instead, it's crucial to prioritize one's passions, interests, and aptitudes while considering the demand and income potential of the chosen career. Pursuing a career that aligns with these factors can lead to long-term career success and personal fulfillment. Ultimately, a career should be viewed as a journey of self-discovery and personal growth rather than simply a means to an end.

The wrong way HOW most people select their career

1. 1) INCOME

    2) DEMAND
    6) INTEREST
    3) STREAM SELECTION
    4) APTITUDE
    5) PERSONALITY

Choosing a career is a crucial decision that requires careful consideration and thought. While most people are aware of the importance of choosing a career based on their interests, many students still find it challenging to identify their passions and develop a career path that aligns with their interests. To help address this issue, career counsellors often recommend a three-pronged approach to career selection, which involves considering one's interests, market demand, and talent. However, after extensive research and analysis of various career-related courses, it has been found that a five-step approach is the most effective and correct way of choosing a career.

The right way of choosing a career; Five-step approach of choosing a career

The five-step approach to choosing a career involves prioritizing five key factors: interest, aptitude, personality, demand, income, and stream selection. **The first** and most important step is to prioritize one's interests and calling. Choosing a career that aligns with one's interests can lead to long-term job satisfaction and fulfillment. Individuals who pursue careers based on their interests are more likely to enjoy their work and be motivated to achieve their goals.

The second step is to consider one's aptitude or natural abilities. Aptitude refers to the innate talents and skills that an individual possesses. Choosing a career that aligns with one's aptitude can help individuals perform well in their job and excel in their fields.

The third step is to consider one's personality. Personality refers to an individual's traits, preferences, and behaviours. Choosing a career that aligns with one's personality can improve work-life balance and help individuals avoid stress and burnout.

The five-step approach to choosing a career

1) INTEREST

2) APTITUDE

3) PERSONALITY
4) DEMAND
5) INCOME
6) STREAM SELECTION

The fourth step is to consider the demand for the chosen career. While it's essential to choose a career that aligns with one's interests and abilities, it's also important to consider the job market's demand. Pursuing a career in a high-demand field can offer better job security and growth opportunities.

The fifth and final step is to consider the income potential of the chosen career. While money should not be the sole motivation for choosing a career, it's essential to consider the income potential of the chosen field. Choosing a career that offers a good income can lead to financial stability and allow individuals to pursue their personal goals and aspirations.

In conclusion, the five-step approach to choosing a career, which involves prioritizing interest, aptitude, personality, demand, income, and stream selection, is the best and most effective way to make informed and fulfilling career choices. By considering these factors and taking the time to research and explore various career options, individuals can make confident decisions about their future and achieve long-term career success and personal fulfillment.

Five Career Stages

5 stages of career choice,

There are several different models of career choice, but one commonly cited framework is the five-stage model proposed by Donald Super. Donald Super was a psychologist who specialized in studying vocational behaviour and career development. His five-stage model of career choice is one of the most widely recognized frameworks in the field of career counselling and has been used to guide career development interventions for individuals of all ages.

The five stages of career choice proposed by Super represent a sequential process of vocational development that individuals go through as they choose and pursue their careers. Super's model has based on the premise that career development is a lifelong process and that individuals will continue to make career-related decisions and adjustments throughout their lives.

The model is intended to provide a framework for understanding the career development process and to guide individuals in making informed decisions about their vocational paths. The five stages of Super's model are not strictly linear, and individuals may move back and forth between the stages as they navigate the complex career choice process. The five stages of career choice are:

1. **Self-assessment**: The first stage of career choice involves taking stock of one's personal qualities, such as interests, values, skills,

and personality traits. This self-assessment process helps individuals identify potential career paths that align with their strengths and preferences.

2. **Career exploration:** Once individuals have a sense of their personal qualities, they can begin exploring different career options. This might involve researching different occupations, talking to people in the field, or taking on internships or part-time jobs to gain experience.

3. **Decision-making:** After exploring different career options, individuals must decide which path to pursue. This decision-making process often involves weighing various factors, such as job prospects, salary, work-life balance, and personal fulfillment.

4. **Career preparation:** Once individuals have decided about their career path, they can begin preparing themselves for the job market. This might involve pursuing additional education or training, building a network of professional contacts, or developing relevant skills and experience.

5. **Career implementation:** The final stage of career choice involves putting one's career plan into action. This might include job hunting, starting a business, or pursuing further education or training. It also involves ongoing self-assessment and adjustment as individuals continue to learn and grow throughout their careers.

In short, the career choice process involves several stages, starting with self-assessment, where individuals identify personal qualities such as interests, values, skills, and personality traits. This helps them align their strengths and preferences with potential career paths. Career exploration involves researching and gaining experience in different career options. After exploring, individuals must decide based on job prospects, salary, work-life balance, and personal fulfillment.

The career preparation stage involves pursuing education or training, building a professional network, and developing relevant skills and experience. Career implementation's final stage consists in putting the career plan into action through job hunting, starting a business, or further education. Ongoing self-assessment and adjustment are also necessary as individuals continue to learn and grow throughout their careers.

Discovering Your Life Goal: A Four-Step Process to Unlock Your Purpose and Passion

Setting and achieving your dreams is a powerful way to create a meaningful and fulfilling life. However, it's important to approach dream setting in a systematic way to ensure that your dreams are grounded in reality and that you have a clear plan for achieving them. Here is a 4-step process to help you make sure whether this aim in life or dream is your passion:

1. **Self-evaluation**

The first step in setting and achieving your dreams is to evaluate yourself. This involves studying your interests, values, personality traits, strengths, and weaknesses. Reflect on your past experiences and what you've learned from them. Consider what makes you happy and fulfilled and what you're good at.

This self-evaluation will help you identify your passions and align your goals with your true self. Self-evaluation is an essential first step in the dream-setting process. By evaluating yourself, you can gain a deeper understanding of who you are, what you want, and what you're capable of achieving. Here are some ways to conduct a thorough self-evaluation:

a. **Study your interests:** Think about what you enjoy doing and what activities make you feel most alive. Consider the hobbies or pastimes that you pursue in your free time. What is it about these activities that you find engaging or fulfilling? These insights can help you identify your passions and interests.

b. **Examine your values:** Consider the things that are most important to you in life. These may include your relationships, career, spirituality, community, or personal growth. Reflect on what you value most and how these values align with your personal goals.

c. **Assess your personality traits:** Reflect on your personality traits and characteristics. Are you outgoing or introverted? Detail-oriented or big picture-oriented? Creative or analytical? Understanding your personality traits can help you identify careers or paths well-suited to your strengths and natural inclinations.

d. **Identify your strengths and weaknesses:** Think about what you're good at and where you may need to improve. Consider your skills, talents, and areas of expertise. Identifying your strengths can help you find a career or path that leverages these abilities while understanding your weaknesses can help you identify areas where you may need to develop new skills.

e. **Reflect on your past experiences:** Look back on your life experiences and the lessons you've learned. Consider your successes and failures, and think about how they have shaped who you are today. This reflection can help you identify your values, passions, and strengths and provide insight into the direction you should take in your future.

Overall, self-evaluation is an ongoing process that can help you make informed decisions about your future. By understanding your interests, values, personality traits, strengths, and weaknesses, you can align your goals with your true self and pursue a fulfilling and meaningful path.

2. Research

Once you have a clear understanding of your interests and abilities, the next step is to research the market, skill sets, salaries, and lifestyles associated with your dream. This involves learning about the industry or field you're interested in, the types of jobs available, and the qualifications required to succeed. Researching the current job market and understanding the demand for your chosen field is also important. By doing your research, you can ensure that your dreams are grounded in reality and that you clearly understand what it will take to achieve them. Research is a crucial step in the dream-setting process. Here are some ways to conduct effective research:

a. **Utilize online resources:** The internet is an excellent source of information for researching careers. You can use websites like LinkedIn, Glassdoor, and Indeed to learn about different job titles, salaries, and job descriptions. You can also watch informational videos on YouTube and read articles and blogs that discuss your desired field.

b. **Read books and publications:** Many books and magazines offer insights into different career fields. You can read biographies of successful people in your area or books that provide information about the industry you're interested in.

c. **Conduct informational interviews:** Reach out to people who are already successful in your desired career field and ask if you can conduct an informational interview with them. During these interviews, you can ask questions about their career path, the skills required, and what it takes to succeed in the field.

d. **Talk to your parents and friends:** Your parents and friends may have insight into your desired career path. They may know someone who works in the field or have experience in a related area. Talking to them can help you better understand what it takes to succeed in your chosen career.

e. **Attend events and job fairs:** Attending industry events and job fairs can help you meet people who work in your desired field and learn about job opportunities. These events can also give you a better sense of the skills and experience required to succeed in your chosen career.

Utilizing these resources allows you to gather valuable information about your desired career path and ensure that your goals are grounded in reality. Research can help you identify the skills and experience you need to acquire and the steps you need to take to achieve your dream.

3. Decision-making

The third step is to decide about pursuing your dream. This involves talking with a career counsellor, coach, mentor, or even your parents. Seeking advice from others can help you gain new perspectives and make an informed decision. Ultimately, the decision must come from within, and you must be honest about your goals and the risks and sacrifices involved. Make sure your decision aligns with your personal values and vision for your life.

The third step is crucial, as it involves deciding to pursue your dream career. This step can be challenging, as it requires you to consider multiple factors and make choices that will impact your future. Seeking guidance and advice from others, such as a career counsellor, coach, or mentor, can help gain new perspectives and insights into the field you're interested in.

a. You need to be honest with yourself about your goals, strengths, and weaknesses, and be willing to take risks and make sacrifices to achieve your dream. This can involve asking yourself several big questions about your life, career, and future plans. It's important to keep in mind that, ultimately, the decision must come from within.

b. One key consideration is whether the career aligns with your personal values and vision for your life. If your values and vision are not in line with your career choice, you may find yourself feeling unfulfilled and unsatisfied in the long run. Another important factor to consider is whether the career path you're considering is a good fit for your personality, interests, and skill set. It's essential to choose a career that allows you to use your natural strengths and abilities and your interests and passions. This can help you stay motivated and engaged in your work and achieve greater success in the long run.

c. It's also important to keep in mind that while the job post and place can keep changing, the domain and required skill set and personality for the job won't change anywhere in the world. Therefore, it's essential to focus on choosing the right domain rather than the specific career or location.

d. In making your decision, weigh the potential risks and sacrifices involved. Pursuing your dream career may require significant investment in terms of time, money, and effort, and you may need to make sacrifices in other areas of your life to achieve your goals. It's important to consider these factors carefully and be realistic about what it will take to achieve your dream.

Ultimately, the decision-making process is a deeply personal, and it's important to take the time to reflect and consider all the factors involved before making a choice. By being honest with yourself, seeking guidance and advice, and making an informed decision, you can set yourself up for a fulfilling and successful career that aligns with your values, interests, and vision for your life.

4. Implementation

The final step is to plan to achieve your dreams. This involves creating both long-term and short-term plans. Set achievable goals and establish a timeline for reaching them. Break down your long-term goals into smaller milestones, and ensure that your short-term goals align with your long-term aspirations. Create a plan that includes the resources you will need, the steps you will take, and the support you will require along the way.

The final step in setting and achieving your dreams is to create an implementation plan. This is where you take all the insights, research, and decisions you've made and create a roadmap for achieving your goals. The implementation phase can be divided into two parts: long-term planning and short-term planning.

a. Long-term planning involves setting big-picture goals that you want to achieve in the future. These goals should align with your dreams, vision, and values. To create long-term plans, ask yourself where you want to be in five, ten, or even twenty years. Consider your career goals, personal life goals, financial goals, and any other areas of your life that are important to you. Be as specific as possible when setting your goals, and make sure they are measurable, realistic, and time-bound.

b. Short-term planning involves breaking down your long-term goals into smaller, actionable steps you can take in the present. These are the building blocks that will help you achieve your long-term goals. Create a timeline for completing each short-term goal, and set deadlines for each step. Make sure that your short-term goals are achievable and specific and that they contribute to your long-term objectives.

c. It's important to be flexible with your plans, as life can be unpredictable. You may need to adjust your plans as circumstances change. However, having a plan in place can help you stay focused and motivated, even when things get tough. It can also help you measure your progress and identify areas where you need to improve.

d. In addition to creating plans, it's important to surround yourself with a support system to help you achieve your dreams. This may include friends, family, mentors, or coaches. They can provide you with guidance, advice, and emotional support. Seek out people who share your values and vision and who can help you overcome challenges and celebrate your successes.

e. In conclusion, achieving your dreams requires hard work and planning. By following a four-step process of self-evaluation, research, decision-making, and implementation, you can create a roadmap for success. Remember to be patient, stay focused, and surround yourself with people who support your dreams.

With dedication and perseverance, you can turn your dreams into reality.

In summary of all the above step, dream setting is an important process that can lead to a fulfilling and meaningful life. By following this 4-step process, you can ensure that your dreams are grounded in reality and that you have a clear plan for achieving them. Remember that the journey towards your goals may not be easy, but with persistence, hard work, and a clear plan, you can make them a reality.

Unlocking Success: A Simple Formula for Setting and Achieving Your Goals

1. **Set a goal**

The first step is to identify a specific and measurable goal that you want to achieve. Your goal should be clear, concise, and achievable. Setting a specific and measurable goal is critical to the goal-setting process. It helps to ensure that you are working towards something concrete and tangible. Here are some tips for setting an effective goal:

a. **Be specific:** A specific goal clearly outlines what you want to achieve. For example, "I want to lose 10 pounds in 3 months" is more precise than "I want to lose weight."

b. **Make it measurable:** A measurable goal can be quantified so that you can track your progress. For example, "I want to save Rs.50,000 in 6 months" is more measurable than "I want to save money."

c. **Make it realistic:** Your goal should be challenging but also achievable. Setting a goal that is too ambitious can be discouraging if you don't make progress towards it. On the other hand, setting a goal that is too easy won't be motivating.

d. **Please write it down:** Writing down your goal makes it more concrete and helps to hold you accountable. Put your plan somewhere visible so that you are reminded of it regularly. Remember that setting a goal is just the first step. The real work comes in creating a plan and taking action towards achieving your goal.

2. **Set a limit/plan**

The second step is to set a limit or create a plan for achieving your goal. Determine what steps you need to take to achieve your goal, and set a deadline for each step. This will help you stay on track and make progress towards your goal.

To expand on this step, it's important to break down your goal into smaller, manageable steps. Start by identifying the major milestones you need to hit to achieve your goal. Then, break those milestones down into smaller tasks or actions that you can take to make progress. For example, if your goal is to run a marathon in six months, your major milestones include completing 5K, 10K, half marathon, and full marathon training runs. Your smaller tasks or actions include finding a training program, scheduling time for regular runs, and gradually increasing your distance and speed.

a. Setting a deadline for each step is also important. Make sure your deadlines are realistic and achievable and build some buffer time in case of unexpected setbacks. This will help you stay focused and motivated and ensure steady progress towards your goal.

b. It's also important to be flexible and adjust your plan as needed. Life is unpredictable, and you may encounter obstacles or opportunities that require you to change your approach. Don't be afraid to revisit and adjust your plan as needed to keep moving forward.

3. **List out your obstacles/problems:**

The third step is to identify the challenges or problems that may prevent you from achieving your goal. Think about the challenges that you may face and list them out. Be honest with yourself about the potential barriers that you may encounter.

Identifying potential obstacles and problems is an important step in achieving your goal. By anticipating these challenges, you can be better prepared to overcome them. When listing your obstacles or problems, it's important to be as specific as possible. This will help you develop effective strategies for addressing each challenge.

For example, if your goal is to start a new business, some potential obstacles or problems could include:

- Limited funding
- Lack of experience in running a business
- Difficulties in finding the right location or employees
- Competition from established businesses
- Regulatory or legal challenges

By listing out these obstacles or problems, you can develop a plan for addressing each one. This may involve researching funding options, seeking advice from experienced entrepreneurs, networking to find the right employees, and understanding relevant laws and regulations. Remember that not all obstacles can be anticipated, but by being proactive in your approach, you can minimize the impact of unforeseen challenges.

4. List out how to solve it.

The fourth step is to devise a plan to overcome the obstacles or problems you have identified. Brainstorm solutions and strategies that will help you overcome each challenge. This will help you be better prepared to face the obstacles and stay on track towards your goal. To list out how to solve the obstacles or problems, you can follow these steps:

a. Take each obstacle or problem that you listed and brainstorm possible solutions. Think creatively and be open to different ideas.

b. Evaluate each solution and consider the potential benefits and drawbacks of each one. Choose the solution most likely to help you overcome the obstacle or problem.

c. Identify the resources and support that you will need to implement the solution. This may include additional training, financial resources, or support from friends or family.

d. Create an action plan for implementing the solution. Break the solution into small, manageable steps and establish a timeline for completing each step.

e. Monitor your progress and adjust your plan as needed. As you work through your plan, be open to feedback and be willing to make changes if necessary. You can create a clear roadmap for overcoming challenges and achieving your goals by listing out how to solve the obstacles or problems.

5. **Start an action**

The final step is to take action towards your goal. Taking action is an essential part of achieving any goal. Use your plan and strategies to overcome obstacles, stay on track, and make progress towards your goal. Celebrate small milestones and stay motivated by reminding yourself of the benefits of achieving your goal. Here are some steps you can take to get started:

a. Break down your goal into smaller, more manageable tasks. This will help you avoid feeling overwhelmed and make it easier to track your progress.

b. Set a timeline for completing each task. This will help you stay on track and ensure that you are making steady progress towards your goal.

c. Identify potential obstacles that you may encounter along the way. Come up with strategies for overcoming these obstacles so that you are better prepared to handle them when they arise.

d. Take the first step towards your goal, no matter how small it may seem. This will help you build momentum and gain confidence as you begin to make progress.

e. Celebrate small milestones along the way. This will help you stay motivated and remind you of your progress towards your goal.

f. Stay focused on the benefits of achieving your goal. Visualize yourself successfully achieving your goal and think about how it will positively impact your life.

g. Remember, taking action towards your goal requires discipline, commitment, and perseverance. Stay focused, stay motivated, and don't give up!

6. Revise, reflect and edit it.

A well-crafted plan is a great starting point when working towards a goal. However, the path to success is rarely straightforward and can be full of twists and turns. That's why it's essential to regularly revise, reflect, and edit your plan. In fact, revising, reflecting, and editing your plan is not just helpful, but it's necessary to ensure that you stay on track and achieve your goals. In this way, it is a critical component of any successful goal-setting strategy. In this article, we'll explore why revising, reflecting, and editing your plan is essential for achieving your goals and provide tips to help you execute this process effectively. Here are some tips to help you with this process:

a. Set aside time regularly to review your plan and assess your progress. This will help you stay on track and identify any changes or adjustments that need to be made.

b. Reflect on your experiences and assess what is working and what is not. This will help you identify areas where you need to adjust your plan and develop new strategies for success.

c. Don't be afraid to make changes to your plan. Your original plan needs to be adjusted as you gain new insights and experiences.

This is a normal part of the process and can help you stay flexible and adaptable.

d. Remember to stay focused on your goal. Even if your plan needs to be adjusted, your ultimate goal should remain the same. Keep this in mind as you make changes to your plan and strategies.

e. Finally, celebrate your successes along the way. This will help you stay motivated and remind you of your progress towards your goal.

f. Remember, revising, reflecting, and editing your plan is key to achieving your goal. Stay flexible, stay focused, and stay committed to your success!

By following these five steps, you can create a simple formula for goal setting that can be applied to any goal you want to achieve. Remember to stay focused, motivated, and committed to achieving your goals.

CAREER GOAL SETTING - 8-STEP PROCESS

1. **Identify your Signature Strength**

Identifying your signature strength is an important step in the career goal-setting process. It involves recognizing the innate qualities that make you unique and valuable in the workforce. Your signature strengths are the traits that come naturally to you, that you frequently use, and that energizes you when you use them. These strengths are integral to who you are and what you have to offer as a professional.

Your signature strength can manifest itself in different ways, depending on the situation. For example, a person with a signature strength of "leadership" may naturally take charge and guide a group of people towards a common goal, whether in work or social settings. Alternatively, a person with a signature strength of "creativity" may enjoy generating new and innovative ideas, whether in an artistic pursuit or in a brainstorming session with colleagues.

By identifying your signature strengths, you can better understand what kind of work you are best suited for and what you find most fulfilling. You can also use this knowledge to explore different career options that resonate with your signature strengths. For example, if your signature strength is "empathy," you might consider pursuing a career in counselling, social work, or another field that involves helping others.

It's important to recognize that your signature strengths are unique to you and may not be the same as those of others. Some people may have a combination of strengths that make them particularly well-suited for certain careers. Others may have signature strengths that are less commonly found in their industry, giving them a competitive advantage in the job market.

Overall, identifying and celebrating your signature strengths can help you build confidence and motivation as you work towards achieving your career goals. It can also help you find both fulfilling and enjoyable work, leading to a more satisfying and successful professional life.

2. **Explore career options that best resonate with your Signature Strength.**

Exploring career options that align with your signature strengths is crucial in achieving career goals. To begin, identify your top signature strengths by reflecting on the traits that you frequently use, and celebrate and that comes naturally to you. You can also seek the input of others to gain a more objective perspective on your strengths.

Once you have identified your signature strengths, the next step is to explore different career options that best resonate with them. Start by gathering basic information about each potential career, such as job duties, required qualifications, and potential salary. You can use various resources, including career guides, online job boards, and job fairs, to help you with this research.

It's also essential to speak with people already working in the fields you are interested in. Consider making a list of known individuals and arranging to meet them to gain an insider's perspective on working in their industry. This information can be invaluable in helping you decide whether a particular career is right for you.

Based on your research and feedback, you should be able to narrow down your list of career options to your top five choices. Take time to weigh the pros and cons of each option and compare them against your goals and priorities. Consider eliminating opportunities that don't align with your values, work style, or long-term career goals.

Finally, it's time to freeze on one career option that best aligns with your signature strengths, values, and goals. This decision should be based on your research, personal values and what you believe will best fit your long-term career aspirations. Remember, this is a process that takes time, effort, and reflection, and it is essential to remain open to new opportunities and adapt to changing circumstances.

3. Choose Stream & Subject Selection based on Career selection.

Choosing the right stream and subject selection is crucial to achieving your career goals. Once you have decided on your career path, it's essential to research the educational requirements and qualifications needed to pursue that particular career. Find out the subjects and academic streams required for your chosen career option.

Based on your research, choose the subjects that align with your career goals and cater to your interests and strengths. You can also seek guidance from a career counsellor or use psychometric tests and personality assessments to understand your aptitude and make informed choices.

Choosing the right stream, such as science, arts, or commerce, is equally important. It should align with your chosen career and the subjects you have opted for. You can also research the career options available in each stream to make an informed decision.

Remember that your chosen stream and subjects play a vital role in your overall academic performance and future career prospects. Hence, take your time, do your research, and make a well-informed decision that will help you achieve your career goals.

4. **Road map-Milestone**

Once you have identified your career path and the necessary stream and subjects, it's time to plan your educational journey. Making a road map is an essential step towards achieving your career goal. Here are some steps to help you create a roadmap:

a. **Identify the best institutions:** Research and identify the top institutions that offer courses related to your chosen career. Look for institutions with a good reputation and a track record of producing successful graduates.

b. **Selection Criteria:** Determine the selection criteria for the institutions you want to apply to. Consider factors such as location, reputation, ranking, faculty, infrastructure, course curriculum, and fees.

c. **Exam Dates:** Identify the dates for relevant entrance exams required for the institutions you want to apply to. Keep track of the application deadline, exam date, and result announcement dates.

d. **Best Coaching Institutes:** If required, research and shortlist the best coaching institutes to prepare for the entrance exams.

e. **Milestones:** Break down the entire admission process into milestones such as registering for the exam, completing the application process, preparing for the exam, appearing for the exam, and applying for admission. Assign a timeline for each milestone and track your progress.

f. **Timelines:** Create a timeline for your entire education journey, including the course duration, internships, and other relevant activities. Plan and track your progress to ensure that you stay on track towards achieving your career goal.

By following these steps, you can create a roadmap that outlines the steps required to achieve your career goal, identify the best institutions for your education, and keep track of your progress towards your ultimate goal.

5. Resource Management-Wheel Of Life.

Resource Management-Wheel Of Life is a tool that helps individuals access and manages different aspects of their lives. This tool is useful in career goal setting, as it helps individuals identify areas that require more attention and resources.

The Wheel of Life is divided into different categories, which can include career, finance, health, relationships, personal growth, and other important aspects of life. Individuals rate each category on a scale from 1 to 10, with 1 indicating a low level of satisfaction and 10 indicating a high level of satisfaction.

By assessing each category, individuals can identify areas where they are doing well and where they need to focus their attention. For example, if an individual rates their career satisfaction at a 7, but their financial satisfaction at a 3, they may need to improve their financial management skills to achieve a more balanced life.

Once individuals have assessed each category, they can develop a plan to improve areas that require more attention. This plan may involve setting specific goals and taking action steps to achieve those goals. For example, if an individual wants to improve their financial management, they may set a goal to save a certain amount of money each month and take steps to reduce their expenses.

The Resource Management-Wheel Of Life tool is valuable in career goal setting, as it helps individuals identify areas that require more attention and resources. Individuals can achieve a more balanced and fulfilling life by developing a plan to improve these areas.

Understanding and prioritizing different aspects of life is important to ensure overall growth and success. This is especially crucial for students who are just starting out in their academic and personal journeys. One effective way to do this is by identifying eight key quadrants to help them achieve their goals.

i. **The first quadrant is Talent.** This refers to any special skill or ability a student may have, such as singing, dancing, mimicry, acting, or playing a musical instrument. Nurturing and developing these talents can help boost their self-esteem and pave the way for future success.

ii. **The second quadrant is Sports.** This includes indoor and outdoor sports activities a student can participate in to stay fit, healthy, and energized. Regular exercise can help them build physical strength and endurance and provide an outlet for stress and anxiety.

iii. **The third quadrant is Health.** This encompasses everything related to a student's physical and mental well-being, including eating habits, fitness routines, and sleep schedules. Adopting healthy habits at an early age can significantly impact their overall health and longevity.

iv. **The fourth quadrant is Family.** This includes spending quality time with family members, playing games, travelling, and having open discussions. A strong family bond can provide a sense of security and support and can be instrumental in helping students navigate the challenges of life.

v. **The fifth quadrant is Friends.** This involves building positive and supportive relationships with peers, sharing experiences, and exploring new things together. Good friendships can help students feel accepted, understood, and valued, and can provide a valuable source of motivation and inspiration.

vi. **The sixth quadrant is Social Responsibility.** This refers to activities that involve giving back to the community, such as tutoring, sharing books or toys with underprivileged children, volunteering, or participating in social and environmental campaigns. Encouraging students to be socially responsible can help them develop empathy, compassion, and a sense of civic duty.

vii. **The seventh quadrant is Studies.** This includes all aspects of academic learning, such as completing homework, revising for exams, and planning study schedules. Effective study habits can help students stay organized, motivated, and on track to achieve their academic goals.

viii. **The eighth and final quadrant is Knowledge & Skills Development.** This involves identifying areas of interest and pursuing learning opportunities to develop new skills and knowledge. Encouraging students to continuously learn and grow can help them stay relevant, adaptable, and successful in today's rapidly changing world.

By identifying these eight quadrants, students can develop a well-rounded approach to life and prioritize the areas that are most important to their growth and success.

6. **Identify your Mentor & Coach.**

Identifying a mentor can be a crucial step in achieving your career goals. A mentor is someone who can provide guidance, advice, and support as you navigate your professional journey. Here are some steps to help you identify and choose the right mentor:

i. **Please determine what you want in a mentor:** Before looking for a mentor, it's important to know what you want from them. Consider what areas of your career you want to develop and what kind of guidance and support you need. Do you want someone who has experience in your field or someone who can help you with general career advice? Do you prefer a hands-on, involved mentor or someone who provides guidance from a distance? Knowing what you want will help you find the right mentor.

ii. **Look for potential mentors:** Once you know what you're looking for, start identifying potential mentors. Look for people with the skills, experience, and knowledge you're looking for and who you admire and respect. This might include people in your current or former workplaces, industry associations or networking events, or even social media platforms.

iii. **Reach out to potential mentors:** Once you've identified potential mentors, it's time to reach out to them. This could involve sending an email or LinkedIn message to introduce yourself, asking to schedule a meeting or phone call, or requesting to shadow them on the job. Be clear about why you're reaching out and what you hope to gain from the relationship.

iv. **Build a relationship with your mentor:** Once you've established a relationship with your mentor, it's important to cultivate it. Set up regular check-ins, communicate openly and honestly about your goals and challenges, and be receptive to feedback and advice. Remember that your mentor is there to support you, but you also need to be an active participant in the relationship.

v. **Show gratitude and give back:** As you benefit from the guidance and support of your mentor, remember to show gratitude and give back. This could involve expressing appreciation for their time and expertise, sharing your knowledge and experiences, or referring them to other mentees who could benefit from their guidance. Building a strong, supportive relationship with your mentor can be key to achieving your career goals.

7. **Time Management.**

Planning & Time Management are crucial skills for achieving one's career goals. To ensure that you are making the most of your time, it is important to establish a plan and use effective time management techniques.

The ABCDE Method of time management is a technique that can help you prioritize tasks and increase your productivity. This method involves assigning a letter to each task on your to-do list based on its level of importance and completing tasks in order of priority. The ABCDE method is a time management technique developed by Brian Tracy, a renowned author and speaker. It is a simple but effective system for managing time, prioritizing tasks, and achieving goals.

The method involves categorizing tasks according to their importance and urgency level and then taking action on each task based on its category. Here's how it works:

- **A:** Tasks that are important and urgent. These are the most pressing tasks that require immediate attention, and you should tackle them first.
- **B:** Tasks that are important but not urgent. These tasks are important for achieving your long-term goals but don't require immediate attention. Schedule these tasks for a later time when you can give them your full attention.
- **C:** Tasks that are urgent but not important. These are tasks that require immediate attention, but they do not contribute to your long-term goals. Try to delegate or eliminate these tasks whenever possible.
- **D:** Tasks that are not important and not urgent. These are low-priority tasks that can be eliminated or postponed.
- **E:** Tasks that can be eliminated altogether. These are tasks that are unnecessary or unimportant, and you can eliminate them without consequence.

By using the ABCDE method, you can prioritize your tasks based on their level of importance and urgency and take action on each task accordingly. This will help you to stay focused on your goals, manage your time more effectively, and achieve greater success in your personal and professional life.

In addition to the ABCDE Method, other time management techniques include:

- Creating a daily or weekly schedule
- Breaking down large tasks into smaller, more manageable parts
- Using technology tools like calendar apps and productivity software
- Setting realistic deadlines and goals for yourself
- Learning to say "no" to non-essential tasks and requests
- Taking breaks and giving yourself time to rest and recharge

Effective time management is essential for achieving your career goals, and the ABCDE Method is just one technique that can help you stay focused and productive.

8. **Review & Improve.**

One important aspect of this step is to review and update one's road map and milestone goals. As circumstances and priorities change, it may be necessary to adjust timelines or adjust specific goals. It is also important to evaluate one's resource management and ensure that one is continuing to invest time and energy into areas that are important for career success. This may involve taking courses or training programs, networking with colleagues, or seeking out new opportunities to develop one's skills and expertise.

Another important aspect of this step is to continue seeking and connecting with mentors and coaches who can provide guidance and support along the way. This can involve seeking feedback and advice from experienced professionals in one's field or connecting with others with similar career goals and aspirations.

Finally, it is essential to regularly review and evaluate one's time management strategies. This may involve utilizing the ABCDE method or other time management tools to ensure that one is prioritizing tasks effectively and making the most of each day. By regularly reviewing and improving each step of the career goal-setting process, individuals can stay on track and make progress towards their ultimate career objectives.

Different types of tests that are important for parents and students

1. MI Psychometric Test

The MI Psychometric Test is a convenient and efficient tool for students in Class 6 and above to gain a better understanding of their multiple intelligence and preferred learning style. The test takes only 15-30 minutes to complete and is available in both online and offline formats. The results are interpreted by a trained counsellor, which takes an additional 20-30 minutes.

While the market price of the test typically ranges from Rs.1000-2500, it is available for a school at a discounted rate of just Rs.250 per student for bulk purchases at my centre. The comprehensive 20-page colour report provides detailed information on multiple aspects of the student's learning and personal preferences, including:

> i. **Understanding of multiple intelligence:** The report analyzes eight different types of multiple intelligence, such as Logical-Mathematical, Musical, Naturalist, Verbal Linguistic, Interpersonal, Bodily-Kinaesthetic, Spatial-Visual, and Intrapersonal. This helps students identify their strengths and weaknesses in various areas and learn about their unique abilities and learning styles.

> ii. **Personalized learning:** The report provides information on each student's preferred learning style, which can help teachers tailor their teaching methods to the individual student. This can lead to more effective learning and improved academic performance.

iii. **Career guidance:** The report includes a Multiple Intelligence Career Chart with over 150 career recommendations, allowing students to explore potential career paths that align with their strengths and interests.

iv. **Self-awareness and personal growth:** The report provides insights into the student's potential and preferences, helping them gain a better understanding of themselves and their personal growth opportunities. The report also includes 25 ways to enhance their Multiple Intelligence, which can help students take proactive steps to improve their skills and overall performance.

Overall, the MI Psychometric Test and the comprehensive report can help students make informed decisions about their education and future career goals. By understanding their strengths and learning preferences, students can take steps to improve their academic performance and personal growth. At just Rs.800 per student at my centre, the MI Psychometric Test is an affordable and valuable investment in a student's future.

After completing the test, you can view your report within a few minutes. We also offer an interpretation session to help you understand your report better. Our team of experts will provide you with detailed insights and guidance to help you make informed decisions about your career path based on your report.

2. Psychometric Career Aptitude Test

The Psychometric Career Aptitude Test is a comprehensive and reliable tool designed to help individuals assess their potential for various career paths. The test is open to anyone from class 6 and above up to 35 years of age, and the report consists of 82 pages filled with insightful information and analysis.

The market price for the test is Rs.3,500, but at our centre, we offer it at a significantly reduced price of Rs.1500. Schools can also take advantage of bulk purchases at Rs. 800 per test, making it an accessible option for students across various economic backgrounds. The test report offers numerous benefits, including over 100 career recommendations. An AI-powered system generates 20 lakh personalized results, ensuring that every individual receives tailored advice and guidance based on their unique strengths and interests.

In addition to career recommendations, the report includes a range of analyses, such as interest score, brain mapping analysis, personality analysis, detailed skill gap analysis, and subject/stream recommendations. The report also provides access to a careers reference map and a list of over 200 top colleges for national and international levels.

The test also includes key quotients such as IQ, PQ, EQ, and SQ, which provide a more in-depth understanding of an individual's strengths and potential areas for improvement. The report also offers access to 4,645 career pathways, including certification, diploma, and degree courses for individuals who have completed class 10, 12, or graduate-level education.

Overall, the Psychometric Career Aptitude Test is a valuable tool for individuals seeking guidance on their career paths. It provides personalized recommendations and detailed analyses that can help individuals make informed decisions about their future.

The Psychometric Career Aptitude Test is a valuable tool for students as it can help them discover their strengths and interests in various career fields. By taking the test, students can gain insight into the career paths that may be most fulfilling and suitable for them, which can help them make informed decisions about their education and future career choices.

The benefits of this test are numerous. For example, it can help students identify their natural strengths, which can be a helpful guide for making decisions about their education and career goals. Additionally, the detailed skill gap analysis can help students understand where they may need to improve their skills or acquire new ones to succeed in their chosen career field.

The career recommendations provided in the test report can also help students explore career options they may not have considered before, while the subject/stream recommendations can guide them in choosing the right academic path. The report's detailed reference map of top colleges and universities can also help students identify the best institutions for their chosen field of study.

Overall, the Psychometric Career Aptitude Test can be a valuable tool for students looking to make informed decisions about their education and career goals. By providing personalized insights into their strengths, interests, and skill gaps, the test can help students make better-informed decisions about their future.

How to: The test is entirely online, and there is no need for any physical meetings. Upon receiving your details, we will create a personalized account for you, and you will receive your login ID and password, along with a link to access the test, via email. Once you have completed the test, you can view your report of 80+ pages within a few minutes. We also offer an interpretation session to help you understand your report better. Our team will provide you with expert guidance and insights to help you make informed decisions about your career path.

3. DMIT Lifetime Test

The DMIT (Dermatoglyphics Multiple Intelligence Test) lifetime test is a comprehensive assessment that can be done by individuals of any age. It is available at a market price of Rs.5,000, but at my centre, you can get it for a more affordable price of Rs.3,000. For bulk purchases, it is available for Rs.2,000 per test for schools and academic Institutions.

The DMIT lifetime test is a scientific way to identify an individual's innate strengths, weaknesses, and natural learning style by analyzing their fingerprints. The test is based on the scientific field of dermatoglyphics, which studies the patterns of ridges and lines on the fingertips and palms of the hands. The test results come in a comprehensive 70-page colour report, providing detailed information about the individual's abilities, personality traits, and learning styles.

Institutions that opt for the DMIT lifetime test can take their teaching system to the next level by incorporating a more scientific and modern approach. I also offer training for teachers to help them understand and utilize the test results to better tailor their teaching methods to each student.

The DMIT lifetime test can greatly benefit parents who want to gain valuable insights into their child's unique strengths and weaknesses. The report includes valuable insights about the child's intelligence, creativity, emotional quotient, and other key factors that can influence their success and well-being. By understanding their child's natural learning style and abilities, parents can make informed decisions about their education and extracurricular activities and provide appropriate support and guidance.

The DMIT lifetime test can be a valuable tool for parents seeking to better understand their child's unique strengths and weaknesses. By providing insights into their child's natural abilities and learning style, parents can help their child reach their full potential and achieve success in their personal and professional lives.

BENEFITS OF DMIT TEST ACCORDING TO AGE GROUPS:
DMIT Test Benefits for kids (Ages 2 years to 12 years)

The DMIT test is an incredibly useful tool for parents of children aged 2 to 12 years, as it offers a range of benefits that can help optimize their child's development. By taking a DMIT test, parents can uncover the unique strengths and abilities of their child, and discover any latent talents or gifts that may be present. This information can be invaluable in helping parents provide the right environment and opportunities for their child to thrive and reach their full potential.

In addition to revealing a child's innate abilities and aptitudes, the DMIT test also provides insights into their personality traits, as well as their left-right brain dominance. Armed with this knowledge, parents can gain a deeper understanding of their child's learning style, and tailor their approach to education accordingly. This can help to optimize their child's academic performance and ensure they are learning in a way that is natural and intuitive to them.

Furthermore, the DMIT test can also help parents overcome the tendency to compare their child to their peers. By recognizing and celebrating their child's unique strengths and abilities, parents can help foster a sense of self-worth and confidence in their child, which can have positive effects on their social and emotional development as well.

Overall, the DMIT test is a valuable tool for parents who want to help their child reach their full potential and can provide a range of benefits for children aged 2 to 12 years.

DMIT Test Benefits for teenagers (Age 12 years to 18 years)

1. *Helps identify strengths and weaknesses in order to choose the right stream:* Teenage years are a crucial period for students as they have to make important decisions regarding their academic and professional life. The DMIT test can help teenagers identify their strengths and weaknesses, which can guide them in selecting the right academic stream. This can lead to better academic performance and career prospects in the long run.

2. *Helps identify the most suitable career path based on strengths and interests:* The DMIT test can also help teenagers discover their natural strengths and interests, which can guide them towards a suitable career path. By identifying their natural abilities, teenagers can make informed decisions about their future career and avoid wasting time and resources pursuing a career that may not be the right fit for them.

3. *Helps develop problem-solving skills and decision-making abilities:* The DMIT test can help teenagers develop problem-solving skills and decision-making abilities by identifying their thinking styles and preferences. By understanding their thinking patterns, teenagers can learn how to approach problems and challenges in a more effective and efficient way, leading to better

decision-making skills.

4. *Helps enhance creativity and emotional intelligence:* The DMIT test can help teenagers enhance their creativity and emotional intelligence by identifying their dominant thinking styles. This can lead to a better understanding of their emotions, and help them manage them effectively. Furthermore, by understanding their thinking patterns, teenagers can learn how to think creatively and come up with innovative solutions to problems.

Overall, the DMIT test can be an effective tool for teenagers to make informed decisions about their academic and professional life, and develop important skills and abilities that can help them succeed in the future.

The benefits of DMIT test for adults aged 18 years and above can be summarized as follows:

1. *Identifying True Potential and Natural Talents:* The DMIT test can help individuals identify their true potential and natural talents, which may have gone unnoticed otherwise. This awareness can help them pursue careers or hobbies that align with their strengths, resulting in a more fulfilling life.

2. *Choosing Appropriate Career Path:* The DMIT test can assist in selecting the most appropriate career path based on an individual's personality and strengths. This can lead to better job satisfaction and success in the chosen career.

3. *Improving Interpersonal Relationships:* The DMIT test helps individuals understand their communication style, enabling them to communicate better with others. This understanding can lead to better interpersonal relationships, both personally and professionally.

4. *Managing Stress and Emotional Intelligence:* By understanding oneself better, the DMIT test can help individuals manage stress and improve their emotional intelligence. This can result in better mental and emotional well-being, leading to a more fulfilling life.

The Benefits of DMIT Report for Parenting Tips:

The benefits of DMIT report for parenting tips are numerous, and can help guide parents in raising well-rounded and successful children. Some of these benefits include:

1. **Understanding the importance of early childhood development:** The DMIT report can help parents understand that 80% of a child's brain develops within the first 10 years of their life. This means that it is crucial for parents to provide their children with various learning experiences and skills during this time to help them develop into well-rounded individuals.

2. **Prioritizing creativity and extracurricular activities:** While academic concepts are important, it is equally important for parents to encourage their children's creativity and engagement in various extracurricular activities. The DMIT report can help parents identify their child's strengths and interests, which can then be used to guide their participation in various activities.

3. **Bridging the generational gap:** As children grow up, it can be difficult for parents to relate to and understand their changing interests and behaviors. The DMIT report can help parents bridge the generational gap by providing insights into their child's personality, learning style, and behavior, which can help them connect better with their child and provide effective parenting tips.

4. **Recognizing and nurturing talent:** Every child is unique and has their own talents and abilities. The DMIT report can help parents and teachers recognize and nurture these talents by providing guidance and laying out roadmaps to help their child prosper in their chosen skills.

By using the DMIT report as a tool, parents can gain valuable insights into their child's development and behavior, and use this knowledge to provide effective parenting tips that can help their child reach their full potential.

My advice to parents

The DMIT test and psychometric tests are crucial for students. Many parents invest a significant amount of money in their child's education, including tuition fees, uniforms, and additional home tuition fees. Some even spend lakhs on competitive coaching to secure their child's future. However, despite all these efforts, many graduates remain unemployed, wasting their time and money. Surprisingly, many parents hesitate to spend a small amount on finding their child's career match.

It is essential to take the initiative while the child is young, as soon as they reach the age of two. Conducting the DMIT test will provide valuable insight into the child's innate qualities, abilities, and career matching. Additionally, when the child reaches class 6, they should take a psychometric test to ensure that they are on the right career path. Investing in DMIT tests is a one-time cost that can guide your child towards a successful career. Investing in the right time can save you from wasting lakhs of rupees later on in your career.

My Client Testimonials and Feedback on the Dmit Lifetime Test and Report Can Be Seen Below:

Principal Testimonials

As the school's principal and parent, I would like to express my strong support for the DMIT (Dermatoglyphics Multiple Intelligence Test) that was recently conducted by Mr Sang at our school. When Mr Sang introduced the DMIT test idea, I was initially sceptical and had many doubts. However, after listening to his persuasive speech during the parent-teacher meeting, I was curious to learn more about the test. Half of the parents who attended the meeting enrolled their kids for the test, including my two sons, and I decided to do the same.

Within a month, Mr Sang had completed the analysis of the participants' fingerprints using three different software and produced comprehensive reports for each student. The reports included information about the student's learning style, brain dominance, leadership style, multiple intelligence, and much more. During the interpretation session, his explanation of the reports was clear and in simple language, making it easy for the parents to understand their children's personalities. To my surprise, the reports were true for my two kids, as their real-life personalities were very different from siblings, which was shown in the reports as well. Other parents also confirmed that the reports were accurate and reflected their children's personalities.

I was impressed by Mr Sang's extra efforts to train our teachers on how to use the student reports and provide guidance on how to best help the students based on their individual strengths and weaknesses. Our school is now better positioned to prepare our students for their futures, as our teachers are better equipped to understand and support their unique needs.

In addition to the benefits for the students, I was also pleased to see that the test was conducted at the school and was available at a special discount, which was highly appreciated by the parents. The school will now have the student reports on file for future reference, which will be incredibly helpful in tracking the student's progress and providing them with the support they need to succeed.

In conclusion, other schools should consider conducting the DMIT test. The benefits for the students, teachers, and parents are numerous, and the insights provided by the test into the student's learning style, brain dominance, leadership style, multiple intelligence, and much more will help shape the future of our students.

Principal,

Chiinsuanching, M.A Psychologist

Little Gems Academy.

Children's Home

As parents and teachers, it can be challenging to fully understand and analyze our kids' personalities, intelligence, brain dominance, and future career options. However, my friend Sang has introduced a new way to bridge this gap by introducing the Dermatoglyphics Multiple Intelligence Test (DMIT) at our Children's Home.

While I was initially skeptical about the test, it turned out to be a game-changer. Sang graciously offered to administer the test to our kids for free, and the results have been beyond my expectations. Having known the children for eight years, the DMIT test not only clearly shows their personalities but also aligns with my understanding of them. It provides them with direction for their future and shows them the way ahead.

For example, one of our children's home's kids was identified to have a dominant personality and kinaesthetic intelligence. The report noted that they enjoy physical activities and sports and would thrive in athletics, dancing, or firefighting careers. These findings align with what we already knew about the child and have been incredibly helpful in providing them with a direction for their future.

The DMIT test works by scanning fingerprints and making several observations. It identifies the child's personality type, whether they have a dominant, influential, steady, or compliant personality. It also observes whether the child is object-driven or concept-driven and an executor or thinker. The test also analyzes their performance on eight multiple intelligence and 19 sub-intelligence areas, including intrapersonal intelligence, logical-mathematical intelligence, linguistic intelligence, musical intelligence, and kinaesthetic intelligence. Additionally, the test displays over 100 career options for the child to explore.

While the test may seem expensive initially, it is an investment in your child's future. Compared to buying toys or clothes that may only last a few months or years, the DMIT test is an investment that will last a lifetime.

As the Hope Children's Home coordinator, I highly recommend the DMIT test to all parents and teachers who care for their child's future. Our children have benefited from the test, and we are satisfied customers. The report generated from the DMIT test was found to be true to the child's qualities, and we are confident that it will provide a clear direction for their future.

Rev. James Lalpu

Coordinator

Hope Children Home, New Lamka

From students' parents' feedback or testimonials:

Feedback on Ginlianthang Guite DMIT Test life report:

DMIT test helps parents identify the strength and weaknesses of our child and not to over-expect from them. It is indeed a reliable test and useful analysis, extremely useful in guiding them through life. A must for everyone. Thank you Sir Lammuansang Tombing.

"The DMIT test, as entrusted by many scientific researchers and psychologists, paved way for young parents to guide their children based on their aptitude, passions and commitment. As a father of a one year - old child, I will ensure the children's learning and holistic development are intact as per the report."

By- Lian Hangluah, Research Scholar

To err is human,"they said, and we have all made mistakes or picked the wrong choice once or more in life. While the outcomes of some of these choices are reversible, some are unfortunately not.

So, in regard to a child's future (career-wise), what if we have something that will help us (caregivers) make the right choices and decisions? What if we have something that will show us what our child is 'good at' or 'weak at' so that we can hone those skills and improve their weak areas?

The Dermatoglyphics Multiple Intelligence Test (DMIT) analyses a child's fingerprints using multiple software. This test shows us the range of a person's intelligence, learning styles, thought process, career options and many more. In this fast-changing world, this is a tool with high credibility and easy to comprehend which will help many parents be able to understand their child better and make better choices for their child's future.

Uprooting a sapling is easier than uprooting a tree, so let us start young and give our children the opportunity we never had.

-By Counsellor Sangmuanching, M.Sc Psychology

NOTICE: Interested in the Dermatoglyphics Multiple Intelligence Test (DMIT) or others psychometric testing for yourself or your child? I offer both in-person and online assessments for individuals aged one year and older for DMIT, and psychometric classes for grades 6 and above. Schools and educational institutions can receive an Rs.2,000 per student in bulk discount. Contact me at 8794970270 or lammuansangtombing@gmail.com to learn more and schedule a session.

4. Job Fitment Test:

A job fitment test, also known as a Candidate Aptitude Test, is an evaluation tool used by employers to determine job candidates' suitability for specific roles. The test aims to assess how well the candidate's skills, abilities, and personality traits match the job requirements.

The job fitment test typically includes various questions and exercises designed to evaluate the candidate's cognitive abilities, such as problem-solving, critical thinking, and decision-making skills. It may also include assessments of the candidate's behavioural traits, such as their work style, communication skills, and attitude towards teamwork.

The results of a job fitment test can be used to identify the best candidates for a specific job and to develop targeted training and development plans for employees to help them improve their skills and performance. It can also help employers reduce the risk of employee turnover by selecting candidates more likely to stay in a job long-term.

For job seekers, taking a job fitment test can provide valuable insights into their strengths and weaknesses relating to a particular job or career path. It helps them identify areas where they may need to improve their skills and helps them better understand which jobs are likely to be a good fit for their personality, work style, and values.

Overall, job fitment tests can be a valuable tool for employers and job seekers. They can help improve job satisfaction and performance, reduce employee turnover, and increase overall productivity and success in the workplace.

"If you know the enemy and know yourself, you need not fear the result of a hundred battles. If you know yourself but not the enemy, for

every victory gained, you will also suffer a defeat. You will succumb in every battle if you know neither the enemy nor yourself."
— Sun Tzu, The Art of War

5. Midbrain activation

Midbrain activation is a concept that has gained popularity in recent years as a way to improve cognitive abilities and learning potential in children and adults. The theory was developed by Dr Makoto Shichida of Japan and is based on the idea that the midbrain, or mesencephalon, can be activated through specific training techniques. He researched and studied for 40 years about this Midbrain Activation and found the solution. He has written over 200 books in his lifetime.

The midbrain is a part of the brain stem responsible for processing auditory, visual, and sensory information. It is active from birth until around the age of five, after which it becomes less active. Dr Shichida's theory posits that midbrain activation is possible up to age 16, with increasing difficulty thereafter. Once the midbrain is activated, it remains so for the rest of our lives. Those over 40 years of age have a lower chance of activating the midbrain and are, therefore, not included in the program.

The Midbrain Activation programme involves a two-day training program that can be attended by children aged 6 to 16 and adults aged 17 to 39 years. The program aims to activate the midbrain using various techniques, including visualization, music, and meditation.

Midbrain activation is a technique that has gained popularity in recent years for its many benefits. Here are five key benefits of midbrain activation that are worth exploring further:

1. **Improved sensory abilities:** One of the primary benefits of midbrain activation is its ability to enhance the five senses of the human body. This is achieved by stimulating the area of the brain responsible for sensory processing, leading to sharper

senses and increased sensory awareness.

2. **Balanced brain hemispheres:** Another benefit of midbrain activation is its ability to balance the left and right hemispheres of the brain. By balancing these two halves, individuals are better able to utilize both their analytical and creative faculties, leading to more well-rounded and effective thinking.

3. **Increased brain connectivity:** Midbrain activation can also help to improve the speed and efficiency with which information is transferred between the two hemispheres of the brain. This leads to faster processing and increased overall brain connectivity.

4. **Improved long-term memory:** A further benefit of midbrain activation is its ability to improve long-term memory. By stimulating the midbrain, individuals are better able to process and retain information, leading to improved memory and recall.

5. **Increased learning speed:** Finally, midbrain activation has been shown to increase learning speed, allowing individuals to learn and absorb new information at a faster pace. This can be particularly beneficial for students or those in professional fields that require ongoing learning and development. Overall, midbrain activation has many potential benefits that are worth considering for those looking to improve their cognitive abilities and overall well-being.

The program also has the potential to improve academic results by 15-20% although this has not been researched or scientifically proven, it was stated by my teacher who is a DMIT practitioner over a decade. Proponents of midbrain activation claim that it can enhance creativity, problem-solving skills, and emotional intelligence, among other benefits.

A minimum of eight children is required to begin the program. Furthermore, the program's cost is high due to its one-time nature, offering lifetime benefits. However, we are willing to negotiate fees based on the economic condition of your district or state.

If you are interested in the midbrain activation program and would like to explore the possibility of doing your child, please get in touch with me. Please note that the program requires a minimum of eight children to begin, and fees are negotiable based on the district's economic condition. Additionally, it is important to approach the program with an open mind and to do your own research before making any decisions.

Please contact me if you have any questions or concerns regarding the program or its benefits. I would be happy to provide more information and discuss potential options for your community.

Here are some other types of psychometric tests that are relevant for students:

1. **Myers-Briggs Type Indicator (MBTI):** This personality test assesses an individual's personality type based on four dichotomies - extraversion/introversion, sensing/intuition, thinking/feeling, and judging/perceiving. The MBTI can help students identify their personality type, which can guide them in making career and education decisions.

2. **Strong Interest Inventory:** This assessment tool helps students identify their interests and how they relate to different careers. The test assesses six areas - realistic, investigative, artistic, social, enterprising, and conventional - and can help students choose a career that aligns with their interests.

3. **Emotional Intelligence (EQ) test:** EQ tests assess an individual's ability to understand and manage their emotions, as well as their ability to understand and communicate with others. EQ tests help students develop self-awareness and empathy, which can be useful in personal and professional relationships.

4. **Cognitive Ability Test:** Cognitive ability tests assess an individual's mental capabilities, such as problem-solving and analytical skills. These tests can help students identify their

strengths and weaknesses in cognitive areas, which can help them make decisions about their education and career path.

5. **Career Values Assessment:** This test helps students identify their personal values and how they relate to their careers. By understanding their values, students can make informed decisions about what type of work environment and career path best fits them.

6. **Temperament Test:** Temperament tests assess an individual's temperament, a set of innate characteristics that influence their behaviour, emotions, and reactions to different situations. The test can help students identify their temperament type and how it relates to their personal and professional life, such as their preferred work style, communication style, and leadership style.

7. **DISC Test:** The DISC test is a personality assessment tool that measures an individual's Dominance, Influence, Steadiness, and Conscientiousness. The test can help students identify their personality type and how it relates to their career path and work environment. For example, a student who scores high in dominance may be well-suited for a leadership role, while a student who scores high in conscientiousness may be well-suited for a career that requires attention to detail and accuracy.

Overall, psychometric tests can be a valuable tool for students to gain self-awareness, identify their strengths and weaknesses, and make informed decisions about their education and career path. By understanding their personality, interests, cognitive abilities, emotional intelligence, and values, students can choose a career path that aligns with their strengths and values, leading to greater job satisfaction and success.

If you're unsure which psychometric test to choose and what reports are required for your child's development, feel free to contact me personally. I can recommend the top three tests that are most relevant to your child and can help them gain a better understanding of themselves, as well as find a suitable career. All assessments can be done online, so don't hesitate to invest in your child's growth and future.

The differences between DMIT test and the psychometric test are:

Psychometric tests and DMIT tests are both widely used tools for individuals seeking guidance on their career paths. While both tests offer valuable insights, they differ in their approach and the information they provide.

One key difference between psychometric tests and DMIT tests is the type of information they offer. A psychometric test provides an assessment of an individual's current abilities, including their cognitive abilities, personality traits, and career interests. This information is based on the individual's responses to the test questions and is used to help guide their career path.

In contrast, a DMIT test provides insights into an individual's inborn qualities and abilities. Specifically, the test examines an individual's fingerprints and other dermatoglyphic markers to identify their innate strengths and weaknesses. The DMIT test can reveal an individual's natural intelligence types, learning style, and potential talents, which can be used to guide their career path and personal development.

Another difference between the two tests is the type of interpretation they require. A psychometric test report typically requires a trained professional to interpret the results accurately. This is because the test examines a range of cognitive and personality traits that require an expert understanding to analyze and interpret.

In contrast, the DMIT test report is often designed to be self-explanatory, with clear explanations of the results and what they mean for an individual's career and personal development. However, it is important to note that it is still recommended to have a trained professional interpret the results to ensure accuracy and provide additional guidance.

Overall, the psychometric test and DMIT test offer different types of insights into an individual's abilities and potential. While the psychometric test assesses current abilities, the DMIT test focuses on innate qualities and abilities. Both tests can be useful in guiding an individual's career and personal development, and it is essential to choose the test that best meets an individual's needs and goals.

My last word, if you don't have an interest or don't know your passion

As someone who has been through the process of discovering my passion and calling, I know how important it is to explore your abilities and interests. If you don't put yourself out there and try new things, you'll never know what you like and dislike. And if you don't have a solid reason to like something, it's easy to oppose everything.

I've learned that it's important to keep looking until you find your calling because if you settle for something you're not passionate about, you'll feel purposeless. Nothing will motivate you enough to work beyond your comfort zone. Nobody is truly lazy; they're just unfulfilled by tasks that don't align with their passions. Everyone has the potential for productivity; they just need to find tasks that align with their passions and fulfill them.

I didn't settle until I found my passion and calling, which made all the difference. Since I started running my own office, I've been working long hours every day, and I love it. I don't have a boss, and no one pushes me to work, but I work because I want to. I could work 10-15 hours daily most of the time, even on weekends, and it never feels like work because I'm doing something that I'm passionate about.

Even during the pandemic lockdown, I kept working at my office. I never felt bored because I learned new things, took certification courses, and read hundreds of books. My work gives me a sense of purpose and satisfaction, and I never feel like quitting to do something else. So you should keep exploring until you find your passion and true calling and don't settle until you do.

The psychometric tests mentioned above are designed to assist you in discovering your interests, skill set, and personality traits that can lead to finding a career that is a good fit for you. If you're unsure about your interests or don't have any, there's no need to sit idle. Contact me as soon as possible, and we'll be happy to assist you.

CHAPTER FIVE

STUDY SKILL: HOW TO READ FASTER AND COMPREHEND BETTER, PROBLEM WITH SLOW READING, SPEED READING EXERCISE

As a person who has learned and benefited from speed reading, I recommend this skill to anyone looking to improve their academic performance and productivity. Before I learned speed reading, I used to struggle with completing reading assignments and research papers on time, as I found it challenging to read through the vast amount of material required quickly. However, after acquiring the speed reading skill, my reading speed increased from 220 words per minute to 700 words per minute for easy concepts. This allowed me to read through books and academic papers in half the time it used to take me previously.

In addition to the time-saving benefits, speed reading also helped me to improve my comprehension and retention of the material. Through skimming, scanning, and summarizing techniques, I could better understand the key concepts and ideas of the material and retain the information more effectively. This helped me perform better on exams and assignments and gave me a deeper understanding of the material I was reading.

I recommend speed reading to any student looking to improve their academic performance, save time, and gain a competitive edge in their future career. With continued practice and dedication, anyone can learn to speed read and experience its many benefits.

Problems with slow reading

This is a common problem that many students and adults face when reading. They tend to read slowly and with little efficiency, leading to difficulties in comprehension, retention, and overall productivity. One of the main issues is that people tend to read using old habits that they learned in elementary school. This often leads to a reading speed of around 250 words per minute, which is inefficient. On the other hand, the mind can process information at a much faster rate of 500 words per minute or more. This means that the mind can become bored while the eyes are still reading at a slower pace, leading to distractions and daydreaming.

These distractions can be detrimental to the overall reading experience, as they can lead to re-reading sentences and paragraphs, making it difficult to understand and remember the material. This can be especially problematic for students who need to read a lot of material in a short amount of time. It can lead to a lack of motivation and confidence in their reading abilities, affecting their academic performance.

To overcome these problems, it is important to learn new reading techniques that can help to improve reading speed, comprehension, and retention. Speed reading is one such technique that can be learned and practised to help students and adults read more efficiently and effectively. By learning to read faster and more efficiently, individuals can save time, increase their understanding of the material, and improve their overall academic and professional performance.

Making the decision to improve your reading speed can have a significant impact on your academic and professional life. Learning and practising speed reading techniques can significantly increase your reading speed and overall efficiency when processing written material. While the initial adjustment period may take some time, the benefits of speed reading can be seen in a relatively short amount of time.

In fact, studies have shown that comprehension rates between slow reading and speed reading are only 5% different after applying the techniques consistently for 3 weeks. This means that you can read faster without sacrificing your understanding of the material, allowing you to cover more ground in less time.

To improve your reading speed, start by researching and practising different techniques such as skimming, scanning, and summarizing. These techniques can help you to read faster while still retaining key information. It is important to practice these techniques consistently over a period of time to see results, so make a commitment to set aside time each day to practice speed reading.

By improving your reading speed, you can save time, increase productivity, and have a competitive edge in your academic and professional pursuits. So, take the first step towards improving your reading speed today and commit to practising speed reading techniques consistently for the next 3 weeks. Let's see some of the benefits of strengthening reading speed are:

1. **Time-saving:** By increasing their reading speed, students can cover more material in less time. This can be especially helpful when studying for exams, working on research papers, or completing assignments with tight deadlines.
2. **Enhanced Concentration:** Speed reading demands a significant level of focus and concentration. As students strive to boost

their reading speed, they can improve their ability to concentrate and ignore distractions, leading to better academic performance. For instance, when your teacher is going to ask you for your notes in 10 minutes, you can read with exceptional speed and concentration. You can even learn lengthy essays that would take you thirty minutes to memorize at home, but you can learn them within just a few minutes at school.

3. **Better Retention:** When speed reading is done properly, it can improve information comprehension and retention. Using techniques such as skimming, scanning, and summarizing, students can better understand the material and remember more of what they've read.

4. **Competitive Advantage:** In today's fast-paced academic and professional world, the ability to read quickly and efficiently is a valuable skill. Students who can speed read may have a competitive advantage over their peers when it comes to studying, completing assignments, and performing well on exams.

5. **Personal Development:** Learning to speed read can be a valuable skill that students can use for the rest of their lives. Whether they are reading for pleasure or work, reading quickly and efficiently can help them stay informed, educated, and engaged in the world around them. Overall, increasing speed reading skills can be a valuable investment for students looking to improve their academic performance, save time, and gain a competitive advantage in their future careers.

Reading speed exercise

The exercise you mentioned is a great way to determine your reading speed and can be useful in tracking your progress as you improve your reading speed skills. To start, open any storybook and begin reading at your normal pace. Set a 3-minute countdown timer and read as much as possible.

Once the timer goes off, count the number of lines you finished reading and then count the number of words in the fourth line you read. Then, multiply the number of words in the fourth line by the total number of lines you read in the 5 minutes. This will give you a rough estimate of how many words you read per minute.

Some of the techniques to improve reading speed are:

1. Using a pacer is one technique that can help you to improve your speed reading skills. A pacer is a tool that you can use to guide your eyes across the page, helping you to avoid subvocalization or mentally pronouncing each word as you read. Training your brain to process words faster can significantly increase your reading speed.

2. Another technique is chunking, which involves grouping words together to read them in larger chunks rather than one word at a time. This can be done by focusing on phrases or groups of words rather than individual words, which can also help to reduce subvocalization.

3. Expanding your peripheral vision is another technique that can help you to read faster. By training your eyes to take in more of the page at once, you can reduce the number of eye movements needed to read a page, which can increase your reading speed.

It's important to note that while these techniques can help you to read faster, it's also important to maintain comprehension and retention of the material. This can be done by practising active reading techniques such as highlighting key points, taking notes, and summarizing what you've read.

With regular practice and dedication, these speed reading techniques can help you significantly increase your reading speed while maintaining comprehension and retention of the material. So, incorporate these techniques into your reading routine and see the difference they can make.

Consistency is key when it comes to improving your speed reading skills. If you're truly committed to improving your reading speed, it's important to do the exercises consistently for at least 30 minutes a day for 3 weeks.

At first, you may find the exercises confusing, and concentrating may be tough. It's important to discipline yourself to stay focused on what you're reading, even if you don't immediately understand it. It's normal to feel frustrated or angry at yourself during this process, but it's important to take it easy and not give up.

As you continue with the exercises, you'll find that your comprehension improves, and by the second week, you'll start to see the benefits of your hard work. By the third week, there won't be much difference in comprehension between your faster speed reading and your normal reading, but you'll have gained much information much quicker.

In fact, after 3 weeks, you may find that your normal reading speed has increased up to 500 words or more. This means that not only will you be able to read faster during your speed reading exercises, but you'll also be able to read faster in your everyday life. So, stick with it and stay committed to the process; you'll see the benefits of speed reading in no time.

You can use many exercises to improve your speed reading skills, but for the sake of simplicity, I will focus on four exercises you can practice consistently for three weeks. To get started, set a 30-minute duration and easy read-only material, such as English language texts, social science material, or novels.

Important Note: Despite its simplicity, this exercise has the power to revolutionize how you read and comprehend your notes. Take it seriously and approach it wholeheartedly. In the first week, focus solely on exercise one. In the second week, incorporate exercises two and three. By the third week, integrate exercise four into your routine.

The first exercise involves using a pen or finger to point wherever you are reading and never taking your hand off. To read faster, move your hand more quickly, and your eyes will adjust to keep up with your hand. After 30 minutes of reading, count how many words you have read using the technique I described above.

The second exercise builds on the first, but this time you will ignore the first and last words of each line (not the sentence). Please don't point to the first and last words in each line; instead, leave them to your peripheral vision to read.

The third exercise follows the same format, but this time, ignore each line's first and last two words and read the middle words.

Finally, in the fourth exercise, ignore each line's first and last three words and read only the middle words, letting your peripheral vision take care of the rest.

At first, you may feel confused and find it hard to concentrate on your reading. You will need to discipline yourself repeatedly to focus on what you read, and you may not understand what you are reading, which can be frustrating. However, with regular practice, you will notice a significant improvement in your comprehension and retention of the material.

By the end of the three weeks, you should be comfortable and proficient at these exercises, and your reading speed should have increased to over 1,000 words per minute. While there are many other techniques and exercises to improve your speed reading skills, consistently practising these four exercises can provide an excellent foundation for building your speed reading ability.

Maria Teresa Calderon from the Philippines claims to have earned the Guinness World Record for World's Fastest Reader at 80,000 words per minute reading speed and 100% comprehension.

- From Wikipedia, the free encyclopaedia.

Learning effective study skills is essential for success in academic pursuits, and numerous mnemonic and study techniques are available to help students learn more efficiently and effectively. While it's impossible to cover every method here, we provide study skill training to students and can offer a comprehensive program to improve their academic performance.

If you're a school or college principal, consider having us train your students in these study skills. Implementing these techniques can significantly improve academic results and take your institution to the next level. Many people have successfully used these same techniques, some even holding Genius World Records for speed reading after practising these skills for decades. Investing in these techniques can provide students with long-lasting benefits and set them up for future success.

MD Ahmed memorized 32 three-digit flash numbers projected on an electronic screen for a second each and recalled them correctly in the same order last October.
– source www.deccanherald.com

How to study better?

To improve your studying habits, follow these three tips. **First,** start by reading your textbook thoroughly. Unlike the notes given by your teacher, the textbook is already organized and does not require you to memorize it word for word. Reading each chapter at least twice before studying the notes will help you understand the material better and make studying the notes easier and faster.

Second, when studying your notes, avoid trying to learn everything all at once. Instead, read and try to comprehend the material, focusing on learning only 50% of it at a time. Take breaks and get some sleep before revisiting the material the next day to cover the remaining 50%. This method allows your brain to process and retain information more effectively, leading to better long-term memory.

Third, remember the importance of revision. Without it, you will forget up to 82% of what you learned within a day. Repetition alone is not enough. You need to revisit the material regularly to ensure that you retain what you learned. Set aside time each week to review and revise the material you covered, and you will find that your knowledge becomes more durable over time.

What is your learning style?

Knowing your learning style is an essential component of successful studying. Each person has a unique way of processing information, and understanding your preferred learning style can make a significant difference in your ability to learn and retain new information. There are three main learning styles: auditory, kinesthetic, and visual.

Auditory learners learn best by listening. If you're an auditory learner, make sure to listen carefully during class lectures. Pay attention to the tone, pitch, and inflection of the speaker's voice. Use repetition to reinforce information in your memory, and try to recite the key points out loud. You can also read out loud and record your voice to listen to before going to bed. Discussing the subject with friends and listening to top performers can also be helpful. If you're a parent of an auditory learner, make sure to give verbal instructions clearly and provide plenty of opportunities for discussion.

Kinaesthetic learners, on the other hand, learn best through movement and touch. If you're a kinaesthetic learner, you may have difficulty sitting still for long periods and may find it challenging to focus on reading or listening for extended periods. Incorporating physical activity into your study routine can help you learn and retain information better. Try taking short breaks to stretch, exercise, or engage in other physical activities. Parents can help their kinaesthetic learner by allowing their child to move while studying, such as by walking or bouncing a ball. Using hands-on activities to learn and understand concepts can also be beneficial.

Visual learners learn best using their eyes and imagination. If you're a visual learner, use images, diagrams, and graphs to help reinforce information in your memory. Color-coding information and highlighting key points can also be helpful. Make sure to look at your book while reading, and visualize your notes and handwriting to aid recall. If you're a parent of a visual learner, demonstrate how to do things visually rather than relying solely on verbal explanations.

By understanding your learning style and developing effective study habits, you can improve your ability to learn and retain new information. With time, effort, and practice, you can become a more effective and efficient student.

What is your Acquiring Method?

Understanding how you acquire information is crucial for effective studying. It helps you plan and strategize your study sessions to maximize your learning potential. There are four different acquiring methods, namely self-cognitive, affective, reflective, and reverse methods. Each method has its unique characteristics that influence how you acquire, process, and retain information.

If you know your acquiring method, you can use it to your advantage by tailoring your study habits accordingly. For instance, if you are a **Self-Cognitive Learner**, you are a self-starter and prefer studying independently. You do not need others to push or motivate you to study. However, you might struggle with group work or study sessions, as you prefer to work alone.

On the other hand, if your acquiring method is **Affective Method**, you are an imitation learner, and you thrive in group settings. You are people-oriented and enjoy working or studying with others. Unlike self-cognitive learners, you may need others to motivate and guide you. The more you are pushed, the higher your chances of success.

The **Reflective Method** involves learning through introspection and self-analysis. If this is your acquiring method, you prefer to spend time thinking about what you have learned and how it applies to your life. You may struggle with immediate application of knowledge and instead prefer to take your time to reflect on it.

Finally, the **Reverse Method** involves learning through practical applications and hands-on experience. If this is your acquiring method, you prefer to learn by doing things and experimenting with the information. You may struggle with abstract concepts and prefer concrete examples to understand complex information.

To determine your acquiring method, you can take the Dermatoglyphics Multiple Intelligence Test (DMIT). It is a scientific tool that assesses your learning style, personality traits, and cognitive abilities. Once you have identified your acquiring method, you can develop a personalized study plan that aligns with your unique learning needs and preferences.

Tips to study better

In addition to understanding your learning style, it's also important to develop effective study habits. Some useful tips for studying more effectively include:

1. **Start with the basics:** The foundation of any subject is crucial for successful learning. Therefore, it is essential to start with the basics and read the textbook before moving on to the teacher's notes. The textbook provides a comprehensive overview of the subject matter and is an excellent starting point to gain a better understanding of the concepts. Moreover, it is comparatively easier to comprehend the textbook than the teacher's notes, which can be brief and cryptic. By reading the textbook first, you can build a strong foundation and follow along with the teacher's lectures more easily.

2. **Break it down:** Trying to learn everything all at once can be overwhelming and lead to burnout. Instead, it is crucial to break down your studying into smaller, more manageable chunks. Focus on one concept or topic at a time and dedicate enough time to understand it before moving on to the next one. It is also essential to take regular breaks to avoid burnout and keep your mind fresh. By breaking down your studying into manageable pieces and taking breaks, you can retain information more effectively and learn more efficiently.

3. **Practice, practice, practice:** Repetition is a key factor in learning and retaining new information. To solidify your understanding of the concepts, it is essential to practice using the material in a variety of ways. For instance, answering questions or writing essays based on the subject matter can help you apply the concepts you have learned. Moreover, practicing

regularly can improve your retention and help you recall the material more efficiently during exams or tests.

4. **Get help when you need it:** Learning is a collaborative process, and it is okay to ask for help when you need it. If you are struggling with a particular concept or topic, seeking guidance from your teacher or a tutor can be helpful. They can provide valuable insights and support, which can help you overcome your learning challenges. Moreover, collaborating with your peers can also be an effective way to learn and retain information. By seeking help when you need it and collaborating with others, you can accelerate your learning and achieve your academic goals more effectively.

Right learning environment

Creating the perfect study environment is essential for effective learning. Just like you wouldn't wear a warm blanket in a hot desert or a T-shirt in cold winter, the environment you choose to study in can greatly affect your ability to learn. Finding the right environment for you can be crucial in determining your success. Some people thrive in a busy, bustling environment, such as a common room with others around. They may find the noise and activity helps them focus and stay motivated. Others may prefer a quieter, more isolated space, free from distractions and interruptions.

If you find that noise and distractions prevent you from concentrating on your reading, it may be best to study alone in a place far from your family or to make adjustments to your routine so that you can study when they are not around. For instance, you can emphasize studying during their sleep hours. It is important to remember that you are solely responsible for your future success or failure, so take the time to find the environment that works best for you and make the necessary adjustments to ensure your learning success.

A cluttered and disorganized study space can be distracting and hinder your learning. Therefore, it is vital to keep your study space clean and clutter-free. An organized study space can help you focus and retain information more effectively. Additionally, using a planner or calendar to keep track of deadlines and assignments can help you stay on top of your workload and avoid last-minute cramming.

HIGH-INCOME SKILLS FOR THE 21ST CENTURY: MASTERING PUBLIC SPEAKING, WRITING, SALES, AND LEADERSHIP FOR CAREER SUCCESS

Improving one's skills is beneficial in many ways. It can lead to increased productivity by performing tasks more efficiently and in less time. Having specific skills can make you a more attractive candidate for job opportunities, resulting in better job prospects and higher earning potential. Developing new skills can boost your confidence and self-esteem, and can help you expand your knowledge and capabilities, leading to personal growth. Learning new skills can also increase creativity and innovation by approaching problems and tasks from different angles. Additionally, communication skills can help you better connect with others, express yourself more effectively, and build stronger relationships. Overall, being skillful can lead to a more fulfilling and successful life.

In the 21st century, there are many high income skills that can help individuals increase their earning potential. Here are some examples:

1. Coding and Web Development

Coding and web development are highly sought-after skills in today's digital age, as businesses and organizations rely heavily on technology to stay competitive. The ability to create and maintain websites, applications, and software is critical in this industry, and skilled coders and web developers are in high demand. Web development involves creating, designing, and maintaining websites using programming languages like HTML, CSS, and JavaScript. Meanwhile, coding consists in writing the instructions or algorithms that make software and applications run. There are many specializations within the field, including full-stack development, front-end development, and back-end development.

If you're interested in pursuing a career in coding and web development, the first step is to acquire the necessary skills and knowledge. This can be done through self-study or by attending a coding boot camp or a college degree program. Many resources are available online, including tutorials, videos, and online courses.

Once you have the necessary skills, it's important to build a portfolio of work to showcase your abilities to potential employers. This can include personal projects or freelance work. Networking is also crucial in this industry, as it helps you connect with other professionals and land job opportunities. Attending industry events, joining professional organizations, and participating in online forums are great ways to build a network.

In terms of career options, there are many paths you can take as a coder or web developer. You can work for a tech company or a startup or as a freelancer, or start your own business. The demand for these skills is only increasing, and a wide range of job opportunities are available. The potential for growth and advancement in this field is also high, making it an attractive option for those looking to start or switch to a career in tech.

1. Digital marketing

Digital marketing has quickly become one of the most important skills in the world of business. As more and more companies transition to online platforms, the need for professionals who can create and execute effective digital marketing strategies has grown. The field of digital marketing is vast, encompassing everything from social media marketing and email campaigns to search engine optimization (SEO) and content creation. Those who possess these skills are highly sought after by companies looking to grow their online presence and reach more customers.

To pursue a career in digital marketing, individuals must first gain the necessary knowledge and skills. This can be achieved through various avenues, including online courses, workshops, and degree programs. It is also essential to stay up to date with the latest trends and technologies in the field, as digital marketing is constantly evolving.

Once an individual has gained the necessary knowledge and skills, various career paths are available. Digital marketing professionals can work for various businesses, from small startups to large corporations, or even freelancers. This flexibility allows individuals to choose the type of work that best fits their lifestyle and interests.

In terms of income potential, digital marketing is a high-income skill that can pay very well. As the demand for digital marketing professionals continues to grow, so does the average salary for those in the field. Those who specialize in areas such as SEO or social media marketing can earn a particularly high wage, especially if they can build a strong reputation and client base. With the right combination of knowledge, skills, and experience, pursuing a digital marketing career can be financially rewarding and personally fulfilling.

3. Data analysis

Data analysis has become an increasingly valuable and in-demand skill in today's business landscape. With the rise of big data, there is a growing need for professionals who can effectively collect, analyze, and interpret large volumes of data. Data analysts are crucial in helping organizations make informed decisions and drive growth. They can help businesses to identify trends and patterns in customer behaviour, track key performance metrics, and forecast future trends.

To pursue a career in data analysis, one can start by gaining a strong foundation in math, statistics, and computer science. There are many online courses and certifications available that can help aspiring data analysts learn programming languages such as SQL and Python, as well as statistical analysis tools like SPSS and R. Networking and seeking internships with companies in industries known for using big data can also be beneficial. Building a portfolio of projects and showcasing the ability to analyze data and present insights can be valuable assets when looking for job opportunities in the field. With the high demand for data analysts, pursuing a career in this field has the potential to lead to a lucrative income and promising career prospects.

4. Designing career

Design is a broad field encompassing many different areas, from graphic design to product design to interior design. With the increasing importance of branding and visual communication, businesses and individuals are seeking out talented designers who can help create eye-catching designs that effectively communicate their message. In the digital design world, web and UX/UI designers are particularly in demand, as they can create websites and digital products that are visually appealing and user-friendly.

To pursue a career in design, developing a strong portfolio showcasing your skills and abilities is important. This can include examples of your previous work and personal projects and designs that demonstrate your creativity and style. Many designers also attend design schools or complete online courses to learn the technical skills and software tools required for their specific design area.

Networking and building connections with other designers and industry professionals are also important in the field of design. Attending design events and conferences, joining professional organizations, and connecting with other designers on social media can all help you to build a network and stay up-to-date on the latest trends and best practices in the industry.

Pursuing a career in design can be a fulfilling and lucrative path for those with a passion for creativity and a willingness to continuously learn and adapt to new technologies and trends.

These are just a few examples of high-income skills that can help individuals increase their earning potential. It's important to note that developing any talent requires time and dedication, but the potential rewards can be significant.

High-Income Skills: Relevant and Valuable for Everyone

Don't be afraid to invest in yourself and your future by learning a high-income skill that aligns with your interests and strengths. Many high-income skills can be relevant to a wide range of people, and I suggest you consider learning at least one. These skills can not only help you earn a good income, but they can also offer you the flexibility to work remotely and be your own boss.

1. Public Speaking Skills

As someone who has given over 300 seminars in different schools and colleges at such a young age, being a public speaker has been an incredibly rewarding and fulfilling experience for me.

I struggled with stage fright and nervousness when I started giving speeches and presentations. However, with time and practice, I overcame my fears and became a confident and effective public speaker. I've now been able to represent my team and my family at various gatherings, and it's been a privilege to share my knowledge and expertise with others.

Through my public speaking skills, I have had the opportunity to speak on many stages and earn respect even from teachers and principals in various schools and colleges. It's an amazing feeling to know that my words have impacted and inspired others.

In fact, my public speaking skills have even caught the media's attention. I've been interviewed twice, once by Angel Vision Channel TV and the second time by Hornbill Cable Network TV, both at a very young age. It's been an honour to be recognized for my abilities and to have the opportunity to share my thoughts and experiences with a wider audience.

Overall, being a public speaker has allowed me to connect with people, share my expertise, and make a difference in the lives of others. It's a challenging but immensely rewarding skill to develop, and I encourage anyone interested in public speaking to pursue it with passion and determination.

a. Benefits of public speaking training for students:

Public speaking training is an incredibly valuable skill for students to develop. Not only does it help them to communicate more effectively, but it can also lead to numerous personal and professional benefits.

One of the primary benefits of public speaking training is improved communication skills. When students receive public speaking training, they learn how to convey their ideas clearly and concisely. They learn how to engage with their audience and how to adapt their message to suit different contexts and audiences. By practising public speaking, students can become better listeners, which is a critical component of effective communication.

Another benefit of public speaking training is increased self-confidence. Public speaking can be intimidating, and it requires a significant amount of courage and self-assurance to stand up in front of a group of people and deliver a speech. However, as students practice their public speaking skills, they become more comfortable with themselves and their abilities. This newfound confidence can translate into greater self-esteem in other areas of their lives and increased success in future academic and professional endeavours.

Additionally, public speaking training can help to enhance critical thinking skills. When students practice public speaking, they must research and analyze the subject matter they are discussing. They must develop well-organized arguments to present to their audience, which requires them to think critically about the topic at hand. This process can improve students' analytical abilities and their ability to present complex ideas in a clear and coherent manner.

Another significant benefit of public speaking training is the development of strong leadership skills. As students become more skilled and confident in public speaking, they can take on more prominent roles in group projects, team meetings, and other collaborative efforts. They learn how to communicate effectively with others and how to inspire and motivate their peers to work together towards a common goal.

Finally, strong public speaking skills are highly valued in the workplace. Students who receive public speaking training may have an advantage in the job market, as they will be better equipped to present themselves and their ideas to potential employers. They may also have better opportunities for internships, scholarships, and other programs that require strong public speaking skills.

In short, public speaking training is a valuable skill for students to develop. It can lead to numerous personal and professional benefits, including improved communication skills, increased self-confidence, enhanced critical thinking abilities, strong leadership skills, and greater success in future academic and professional endeavours.

b. **Public speaking income potential:**

Public speaking is a valuable skill that can lead to numerous personal and professional benefits. Among these benefits is the potential for increased income, as strong public speaking skills are highly valued in various industries.

One benefit of public speaking skills is that they can help individuals advance their careers. For example, individuals who can effectively communicate their ideas and engage their audience may be more likely to receive promotions or job offers. They may also be more successful in their work, as they can collaborate effectively with colleagues and build strong relationships with clients and customers.

Another benefit of public speaking skills is that they can lead to opportunities for entrepreneurship. Individuals with strong public speaking skills can leverage their expertise to start businesses or offer consulting services. They can market themselves as experts in their field and offer a fee for keynote speeches or other presentations. This can provide an additional stream of income and greater financial stability.

In addition to these benefits, strong public speaking skills can also increase an individual's earning potential. Some business companies are willing to pay a public speaker who can effectively communicate their message to clients, customers, or other stakeholders. This can lead to higher salaries, bonuses, and other financial rewards.

Finally, individuals with strong public speaking skills can leverage their expertise to create and sell their own products, such as online courses or informational products. These products can provide a passive income stream that allows individuals to earn money even when they are not actively speaking.

Overall, public speaking skills have the potential to increase an individual's income and provide greater financial stability. Individuals with strong public speaking skills may be better positioned to succeed and achieve their financial goals through career advancement, entrepreneurship, or other opportunities.

c. Kind request to the reader

Public speaking is an important skill, whether you're presenting to a large audience, speaking to a small group of colleagues, or even having a conversation with a friend. However, many people struggle with stage fright and find it difficult to speak confidently in front of others. This is where public speaking training can help.

One of the most important things you will learn in public speaking training is how to overcome stage fright. Stage fright is a common experience and can range from mild anxiety to extreme panic. However, with the right tools and techniques, it is possible to overcome stage fright and deliver a powerful and effective speech. Public speaking training will teach you techniques such as deep breathing, visualization, and positive self-talk, which can help you manage your nerves and speak confidently.

In addition to overcoming stage fright, public speaking training will teach you how to open and end your speech effectively. The opening of your speech is crucial, as it sets the tone for the rest of your presentation and can capture your audience's attention. The ending of your speech is just as important as it leaves a lasting impression on your audience and reinforces your message. Public speaking training will teach you how to craft compelling openings and endings that will engage your audience and make your message memorable.

Preparing and writing a speech can seem daunting, but it can be a rewarding experience with some preparation and organization.

The first step is to determine the purpose of your speech. Is it to inform, persuade, or entertain your audience? This will help you decide on the tone and content of your speech. Once you know your purpose, it's important to consider your audience. Who are they? What do they already know about the topic? What do they want to learn? This will help you tailor your speech to their needs and interests.

To prepare for your speech:

a. Research your topic thoroughly.
b. Think about the main points you want to make and how you can support them with evidence or examples.
c. Use credible sources and take notes to organize your thoughts. Once you have a solid outline, start writing your speech.

When writing your speech, keep in mind that you want to engage your audience from the beginning. Start with a strong opening that captures the audience's attention and sets the tone for the rest of the speech. You can use a story, quote, or anecdote to pique their interest. Then, introduce the topic and explain its relevance to your audience. Another key component of public speaking is using various voices and body language. Your voice and body language can convey a lot of information to your audience, and using a variety of tones and gestures can help you emphasize key points and keep your audience engaged. Public speaking training will teach you how to use your voice and body language effectively to convey your message and connect with your audience.

Finally, public speaking training will adjust to the needs of the participants. Everyone has a unique style and strength in public speaking, and public speaking training will help you identify and develop those strengths. Whether you need help with delivery, organization, or content development, public speaking training can be tailored to your specific needs to help you become a more effective and confident public speaker.

Overall, public speaking is an important skill to have, both in your personal and professional life. With the right training and techniques, you can overcome stage fright, open and end your speeches effectively, use a variety of voices and body language, and develop your own unique style of public speaking. So, if you're ready to take your public speaking skills to the next level, consider enrolling in my public speaking training program today.

2. Book writing skill

As someone who has written multiple books, each book gets easier to write with experience. When I wrote my first book, I was nervous and unsure of my writing abilities. But as I continued writing and publishing more books, my confidence grew, and I became more comfortable with the writing process.

One of the greatest benefits of being an author is the ability to share your experiences and knowledge with others. Through my books, I have been able to share my insights and expertise on various topics, such as public speaking, entrepreneurship, and personal development. It's incredibly fulfilling to know that my writing has helped others to improve their lives and achieve their goals.

In addition, writing books can also be a source of income. During the COVID-19 lockdown, when I couldn't open my office or do business, I had a debt of about 2 lakhs. However, I decided to use my time and writing skills to my advantage. I wrote my first book, 'Public Speaking Siam Diingdan,' intending to clear my debts. And to my delight, I could sell 900 copies in the first month, which allowed me to clear my debts for printing the book and my debts during the lockdown.

Overall, being an author has been a rewarding and fulfilling experience for me. It has allowed me to share my experiences and knowledge with others while providing a source of income. And with each book that I write, I continue to grow and improve as a writer. Let me share with you how being an author could help you find a job better and faster than anyone else:

Firstly, it can demonstrate a high level of discipline, commitment, and dedication. Writing a book takes time, effort, and creativity, and having the ability to complete such a project can show potential employers that the candidate can set goals and see them through to completion.

Secondly, publishing a book can showcase a person's expertise and knowledge on a particular subject. This can be particularly useful for jobs that require specialized skills or knowledge. For example, someone who has written a book on a specific industry or topic may be considered an expert in that field and could be hired for related jobs.

Thirdly, publishing a book can help build a personal brand and a following. This can be useful for jobs that require a strong online presence or social media skills. Employers may be interested in candidates with a strong online following, as it can demonstrate that they can connect with and influence others. Overall, being a published book author can be a valuable asset when looking for a job, as it demonstrates a wide range of skills and qualities employers may be looking for.

Let's separate book writing into two;

1. **Non-fiction book author:**

Book writing is a valuable high-income skill in the 21st century, particularly in the realm of non-fiction. By possessing the craft of book writing, individuals can leverage their expertise and knowledge to create content that resonates with their target audience. With the rise of self-publishing and the proliferation of online platforms, there has never been a better time to be a non-fiction author.

Writing a non-fiction book requires specific skills, including research, organization, writing, and editing. These skills can be developed through practice and education and honed over time. Once a book is written, individuals can monetize their work through various channels, including traditional publishing, self-publishing, and online courses.

In the non-fiction world, authors who can write about niche topics or offer unique insights are highly sought after. By establishing themselves as an authority in their field, authors can create a strong following and command high fees for speaking engagements, consultations, and other services.

While book writing can be a challenging and time-consuming process, it is a skill that can provide significant returns for those who are willing to put in the effort. With dedication and perseverance, individuals who possess the skill of non-fiction book writing can create valuable content that resonates with their audience and provides a substantial income stream.

2. Fiction book author

Fiction writing is a high-income skill that requires a combination of creativity, imagination, and storytelling ability. Those who possess this skill and can write captivating and engaging stories have the potential to make a significant income from their work. Fiction writers can earn money through various channels, including book sales, movie and television adaptations, and even merchandise sales. Many successful fiction writers have built their own brands and have become household names, with loyal fans eagerly anticipating their next release.

To be a successful fiction writer, one must have a passion for storytelling and a deep understanding of the elements of fiction writing, such as plot, character development, dialogue, and world-building. It's also important to have a strong grasp of language and writing mechanics, such as grammar and punctuation.

While it can be challenging to break into the world of fiction writing, there are many resources available to help aspiring writers improve their craft and build their audience. Writing communities, workshops, and online courses can provide valuable feedback and support, and self-publishing platforms have made it easier than ever to get your work in front of readers.

Overall, fiction writing is a high-income skill that requires dedication, persistence, and a willingness to take risks and put your work out into the world. But for those who are willing to put in the effort, the rewards can be substantial, both financially and creatively. Learning the craft of fiction writing involves mastering a unique set of rules and techniques. With diligent effort and practice, anyone can become a published author. Similarly, acquiring the skills necessary for writing non-fiction is a valuable and long-lasting investment. Once you have honed your craft, you will be able to apply those skills repeatedly throughout your life, resulting in the ability to produce multiple works of fiction. So, if you're ready to take your book writing skills to the next level, consider enrolling in my book writing skill training program today.

The Art of Ghostwriting: How Professional Writers Craft Books and Articles on Behalf of Others

Ghostwriting is a service where a professional writer writes a book, article, or other content on behalf of someone else, typically the work's author. The client pays a large sum of money to the writer to write the book; in return, the client owns all the rights to the finished product. The writer is a hired hand, working closely with the client to produce work that meets their specifications. The writer may be responsible for all aspects of the book, including researching, writing, editing, and formatting. The writing style and voice are crafted to match the client's perspective, with the writer acting as a tool to bring their ideas to life.

As an experienced ghostwriter, I am well aware of the advantages of pursuing a career in ghostwriting. It can be a lucrative career for those with strong writing skills, as it often involves writing for high-profile clients, such as celebrities or public figures. It is also a great opportunity for writers who enjoy collaboration and the challenge of bringing someone else's vision to life. To pursue a career in ghostwriting, it is important to have strong writing skills, the ability to adapt to different styles and voices, and excellent communication and collaboration skills. Building a network and establishing a reputation as a reliable and talented ghostwriter can also help to attract new clients and secure ongoing work.

As a ghostwriter, I had the privilege of working on a project that allowed me to showcase my writing skills and creativity without putting my name on the finished product. While it may seem like a disadvantage to not receive credit for your work, ghostwriting can be a lucrative and fulfilling career choice.

As a ghostwriter, you are essentially a "ghost" behind the scenes, working closely with the client to bring their vision to life. This can be a rewarding experience as you collaborate with someone to help them achieve their dream of becoming a published author. It also allows you to work on a wide range of topics and genres, from memoirs and biographies to fiction and non-fiction books. The key to successful ghostwriting is clear communication and building a strong working relationship with the client. This involves discussing and agreeing on the project scope, deadlines, and fees upfront and ensuring that both parties are aligned on the project's creative direction.

While ghostwriting can be challenging, it can also be highly rewarding. Not only do you get to help others achieve their goals and bring their stories to life, but you also get paid for your skills and expertise. If you are a skilled writer with a passion for storytelling and a desire to help others achieve their dreams, ghostwriting may be the career for you.

Copywriting as a Lucrative Career: An Overview and Guide to Pursue It

Copywriting is the art of writing persuasive and compelling text for advertising or marketing purposes. A copywriter's main goal is to influence the reader to take a specific action, such as purchasing a product or service. This skill is highly in demand, and it can be a lucrative career for those with excellent writing abilities and a creative mind.

Copywriting can be pursued in various ways, including freelancing, working for an agency, or being in-house at a company.

To become a successful copywriter, it is essential to develop strong writing skills, have a good understanding of marketing principles, and be able to adapt to different writing styles and tones. In addition, learning the basics of SEO can be helpful, as many copywriting jobs involve creating content for websites.

Freelance copywriters can earn a substantial income by offering their services to various clients, while those working for an agency or in-house can earn a steady salary with benefits. Building a portfolio of work and networking with potential clients or employers can help to grow a copywriting career. Overall, copywriting is an exciting and creative career path that can offer financial stability and opportunities for growth.

Sales Skill: The Benefits of Learning Sales Skills for Students

Sales skill refers to the ability to persuade, influence, and convince people to buy a product or service. This is an essential skill for anyone who works in business, from sales representatives to business owners, and it can be highly beneficial for students to learn as well. Students can learn how to communicate more effectively, think strategically, and build relationships with others by developing sales skills.

One of the key benefits of learning sales skills is the ability to communicate more effectively. To succeed in sales, one must be able to clearly articulate the benefits of a product or service, listen actively to the customer's needs, and respond to objections in a way that overcomes them. These skills are highly valuable in various contexts, from job interviews to personal relationships.

In addition to communication skills, learning sales skills can also help students think more strategically. Sales professionals must be able to identify potential customers, analyze market trends, and make decisions based on data and insights. These skills can be applied to various industries and can be highly valuable for students interested in entrepreneurship or business management.

Finally, learning sales skills can help students build relationships with others. Sales professionals must be able to connect with customers on a personal level, understand their needs and preferences, and develop a sense of trust and rapport. These skills can be highly valuable in personal and professional settings, allowing students to build meaningful relationships that can last a lifetime.

Overall, learning sales skills can be highly beneficial for students, providing them with the tools they need to communicate effectively, think strategically, and build relationships with others. By mastering the art of sales, students can gain a competitive edge in the job market and set themselves up for success in whatever career they choose.

CHAPTER SEVEN

THE ENTREPRENEUR'S JOURNEY: BUILDING SUCCESS IN EDUPRENEUR, TRADING, MANUFACTURING, AND MORE FOR A FULFILLING LIFE AND CAREER

As someone who grew up in a community with a high value on education and desire govt. job, I can relate to the idea that most children are trained to become employees rather than entrepreneurs. From a young age, I was encouraged to do well in school and pursue a career in a well-respected profession like medical or engineering. Many of my peers also had similar aspirations, and becoming an employee was the only path to success.

However, as I grew older and gained more experience, I began to realize that entrepreneurship is also a viable and rewarding career path. While it may not be as commonly discussed or encouraged as employment, starting a business can be a way to create something unique and make a meaningful impact on the world.

In fact, more emphasis should be placed on entrepreneurship as a viable career option, as it can lead to job creation and economic growth in our towns and cities. By supporting and encouraging those with the heart and personality for entrepreneurship, we can foster a culture of innovation and creativity that can benefit us all.

While becoming an employee is a common and respectable career path, more attention should be given to entrepreneurship as a viable and rewarding option. If you have the heart and personality for it, I encourage you to pursue your entrepreneurial dreams and make a positive impact on the world.

Choose which domain you wish to work on white collar or blue collar

The choice between a white-collar job and a blue-collar job ultimately depends on an individual's interests, skills, and priorities. Both types of jobs offer unique benefits and drawbacks.

White-collar jobs typically refer to professional, managerial, or administrative roles in industries such as finance, law, healthcare, and technology. These jobs usually require higher levels of education and training and often involve working in an office environment. White-collar jobs often provide higher salaries, benefits, and security than blue-collar jobs. They also typically offer more opportunities for career advancement and personal growth.

On the other hand, blue-collar jobs typically refer to manual labour or skilled trades, such as construction, manufacturing, or transportation. These jobs often require physical labour and specialized training but may not require as much formal education as white-collar jobs. Blue-collar jobs can be more physically demanding but may offer more hands-on and practical work experience. These jobs also offer a strong sense of camaraderie and job satisfaction and may provide opportunities for entrepreneurship.

In summary, both white and blue-collar jobs have unique benefits and drawbacks, and the decision between them ultimately depends on an individual's interests, skills, and priorities. Choosing a career path that aligns with one's values and strengths and provides a sense of fulfillment and purpose is important.

The Red Ocean vs Blue Ocean business; choose one

The Red Ocean and Blue Ocean are two different strategies businesses can use to compete in the market.

The Red Ocean strategy refers to traditional competing in the market. It is characterized by intense competition among existing players in the same industry. In a Red Ocean strategy, businesses try to gain a competitive advantage by offering better products or services, lowering prices, and increasing efficiency. The result is often a crowded market with limited growth opportunities, as companies are fighting over the same customers and resources.

In a blue ocean strategy, businesses look beyond the existing market boundaries and create new markets or industries by offering a unique value proposition that is not currently available. This involves innovating and creating something entirely new that can attract new customers who were previously outside the market. This strategy is characterized by less competition, higher profits, and a focus on creating and capturing new demand. Blue ocean strategy, however, creates uncontested market space and makes competition irrelevant.

The key difference between the two strategies is that the Red Ocean focuses on competing within an existing market, while the blue ocean strategy is about creating a new market. While the Red Ocean strategy can sometimes be effective, it often leads to a zero-sum game. The only way to gain a competitive advantage is by taking away from existing competitors. In contrast, the blue ocean strategy focuses on creating new demand, expanding the market size and creating new growth opportunities.

In short: businesses that adopt the Red Ocean strategy tend to compete within an existing market, while those that embrace the blue ocean strategy seek to create new markets or industries. The choice between the two ultimately depends on the nature of the business, the market conditions, and the organization's strategic goals.

Before taking a decision consider this

Becoming an entrepreneur is a life-changing decision that requires careful consideration. While entrepreneurship can be a highly rewarding path, it's also important to be aware of the risks and challenges involved.

One of the most important factors to consider is whether entrepreneurship suits your personality and interests. Not everyone is cut out to be an entrepreneur, and it's important to have a passion for what you're doing in order to succeed. The most successful entrepreneurs are often those who are deeply committed to serving their communities, solving problems, or creating new products or services that make a positive impact.

Another important consideration is the level of risk involved. Starting a new business is inherently risky, and there's no guarantee of success. In fact, it's estimated that around 65% of businesses fail within 10 years, with approximately 20% failing within the first two years of operation. This means that if you decide to become an entrepreneur, you need to be willing to take on a significant amount of risk and be prepared to face challenges and setbacks along the way.

It's also important to understand that entrepreneurship requires a deep commitment and a strong sense of purpose beyond just the desire for financial gain. Successful entrepreneurs are often motivated by a desire to solve a problem, help their community, or create something that positively impacts the world. If you're motivated solely by the desire to get rich, you're unlikely to succeed in the long run.

Ultimately, becoming an entrepreneur requires a willingness to take on challenges, persevere in the face of obstacles, and continue learning and adapting over time. It's a path that requires a high level of dedication and commitment but can also be incredibly rewarding for those who are willing to put in the effort.

My calling for edupreneur

Allow me to share my personal story as an edupreneur so that you can gain insight into the reality of this profession. In 2015, I went through a deep depression and attempted suicide twice. Thankfully, I survived, and this experience led me to realize that academic knowledge alone was not enough to help me in real life. As a result, I began to discover my passion for edupreneur.

I started reading books outside of my school syllabus and began conducting my own personal observations and researching how I could positively impact my community. I began giving seminars and training sessions, focusing on skill development and personal growth. My focus shifted towards thinking big, and my aim was to bring development to northeast India through edupreneur i.e through seminars and skill training programme.

Between 2015 and 2017, I dedicated myself to personal growth and improvement so that I could become a blessing to my community. In 2016, I began putting my ideas down on paper and conducted interviews with people to gain insights and learn important life lessons. Although it was just a dream and a wish back then, after 8 years, those aspirations became a reality.

My journey as an edupreneur has taught me that true success and fulfillment can only be achieved when you follow your calling and pursue your passions with dedication and persistence. In 2020, I rented an office and started giving professional training sessions for a fee. It has been a challenging journey, but it has been incredibly rewarding to see my work's positive impact on others.

At the start of my business, there was a time when I found myself without any money to buy food. I had experienced not having anything to eat and going hungry for 5 days continuously. I remember going for an entire month without cooking anything and relying on the kindness of my relatives to feed me on the weekends. It was a very difficult time for me, and I often had sleepless nights due to hunger. But I tried to satisfy myself with just water. I had set my tears twice on my edupreneur journey (My passion).

As time passed, I managed to earn a small amount of money, and I started eating once a day. By the third month, I could finally eat like a normal person, with regular meals morning and evening. However, I couldn't afford food in the first month because my plans had failed, and I didn't earn a penny.

Many of my relatives and my family offered to help me during this time, but I refused their offers. I knew that in order to succeed in life, I needed to break the habit of depending on others. I realized that I needed to handle stress and live with debt for not just one or two months but for years and years.

Coming from a poor family, an orphan, and a mother who was a door-to-door vegetable vendor, I understood the importance of having a strong character and mindset. I would have given up a long time ago if I had a weak mindset or character. I realized that entrepreneurship is not just about having an idea but also about having the passion, mental strength, character, and burning desire to serve the community. This is true for me as I could give over 200 free seminars to many schools, Children's homes, Rehab centres, and churches over 3 years. It was only after 3 years that I charged my seminar fee, and according to requirements, I support children's Homes and will continue to do so.

So, if you are thinking of starting a business, ask yourself these questions: Do you have a passion for it? Are you mentally strong enough to handle the challenges that come with it? Do you have the right character to face failures and setbacks? Do you have the desire to serve your community, and are you willing to work for the rest of your life, even if you don't get paid, just because you love what you do? These are the qualities that will help you succeed in business and in life.

Difference between job and entrepreneur

1. **JOB= Just Obey the Boss; entrepreneur is the boss:** In a job, an individual is required to work for someone else and follow their rules, procedures and directions. They are not in charge of the business decisions but instead follow the orders of their employer. On the other hand, an entrepreneur is a boss responsible for making all the business decisions and determining the company's direction.
2. **Job is the employee, entrepreneur is the employer:** As an employee, one is hired to work for a company, and their role and responsibilities are typically defined by their job description. Entrepreneur creates their own business and hires others to work for them.
3. **Job has fixed salary, entrepreneur has income:** A job provides a regular, fixed salary or hourly wage to the employee. However, entrepreneurs can have income from multiple sources, such as sales revenue, investments, or other income streams.
4. **Job is secure, entrepreneur is risky till the 7 years from the start:** A job may provide a sense of security and stability, while entrepreneurship involves a higher level of risk. For the first few years of starting a business, an entrepreneur may not see profits and face significant financial risks.
5. **Job has fixed working hours; entrepreneur can work where he wants, with whom he wants and when he wants:** Employees

typically have fixed working hours and may not be free to choose when and where they work. Entrepreneur, on the other hand, has the flexibility to work from wherever and whenever they want.

6. **Job received less respect than entrepreneur:** Society often views entrepreneurs as successful and risk-takers who are creating something new, while employees may receive less recognition and respect.

7. **Job will never create wealth only living, entrepreneur has the potential to create wealth:** A job typically provides a salary that covers living expenses, but it is unlikely to make significant wealth. An entrepreneur has the potential to create a successful business that generates substantial income and wealth. Yes, it is also depending on what type of business you perform.

8. **Job needs an academic certificate and selection, but an entrepreneur needs strong character:** To get a job, one typically needs academic qualifications and may have to undergo a selection process. However, entrepreneurship requires a strong personality, mindset, and willingness to take risks and persevere through challenges.

9. **Job need to work till pension age 65, entrepreneur can have pension in 35 age:** Most people work until retirement age (around 65) and rely on a pension for income in their later years. However, a successful entrepreneur can retire with a comfortable pension at a younger age, such as 35, if they build a profitable business.

Here's a bit more information about each of the different types of entrepreneurs:

    1. **Edupreneur business**

An edupreneur is an entrepreneur who focuses on creating new and innovative products and services in the education industry. This can include things like online learning platforms, educational apps, personalized tutoring services, and more. Edupreneurs often have a deep passion for education and seek to improve the ways in which people learn and develop new skills.

The education industry is constantly evolving, and there are many opportunities to create new and innovative products and services. To be successful as an edupreneur, it is important to understand the industry and the challenges that exist within it. Here are some tips to help you be a successful edupreneur:

i. **Identify a problem:** The first step in creating an innovative product or service is to identify a problem that exists in the education industry. Research the industry, and talk to educators, students, and parents to understand their challenges and think of ways to solve them. Look for gaps in the market, areas where current solutions are inadequate, or where there is a need for a new approach.

ii. **Develop a unique solution:** Once you have identified a problem, create a unique solution that addresses it. Think outside the box and come up with creative ways to solve the problem. Consider using technology to create an innovative solution, and consider how to make your product or service stand out from the competition.

iii. **Validate your idea:** Before investing time and resources into your idea, validate it by testing it out. Conduct market research to see if there is a demand for your product or service. Test your product with a small group of users and get feedback on how to improve it. This feedback will be invaluable in improving your product or service.

iv. **Create a strong brand:** As an edupreneur, it is important to create a strong brand that resonates with your target audience. Your brand should communicate your values and the value that you offer to your customers. Develop a unique brand identity, including a logo, colour scheme, and messaging that sets you apart from your competitors.

v. **Build a strong team:** Building a strong team is crucial to the success of your business. Hire people who share your passion for education and have the skills necessary to help you grow your business. You may need developers, marketers, customer support, and other professionals to help you create and sell your product.

vi. **Network and collaborate:** Connect with other edupreneurs, educators, and industry experts to learn from their experiences and get feedback on your product or service. Attend conferences, join industry groups, and participate in online forums to expand your network. Collaborate with others to create new opportunities for your business.

vii. **Continuously improve:** The education industry is constantly evolving, so it is important to stay up to date with the latest trends and developments. Stay on top of emerging technologies and new teaching methods, and incorporate them into your offering when appropriate. Continuously improve your product or service based on customer feedback and industry changes.

viii. **Have a strong business plan:** As with any business, it is important to have a strong business plan that outlines your goals, target market, marketing and sales strategies, financial projections, and more. Your business plan will help you stay focused and guide your decision-making as you grow your business.

ix. **Stay passionate and committed:** Finally, staying passionate and committed to your vision for improving education is important. Starting and growing a business is hard work, and you will face challenges and setbacks along the way. But if you stay committed to your vision and keep your passion for education at the forefront of your work, you will be more likely to succeed.

2. **Trader business**

Traders are entrepreneurs who buy and sell goods. This can include retailers who sell products directly to consumers or wholesalers who purchase products in bulk and sell them to retailers. To be successful as a trader, it is important to understand the industry and the challenges that exist within it. Traders must have a good understanding of the market they operate in and strong negotiation and marketing skills to succeed. Here are some tips to help you be a successful trader:

i. **Understand the market:** The first step in becoming a successful trader is understanding the market you are operating. Research the market, its trends, and its players. Understand what products are in demand and who your competitors are. This will help you identify opportunities and stay ahead of the curve.

ii. **Develop a niche:** Once you have a good understanding of the market, consider developing a niche. This will allow you to focus your efforts on a specific market segment, which can help you differentiate yourself from your competitors. For example, you could focus on selling products to a particular demographic, such as children or seniors, or on a specific product category, such as electronics or home goods.

iii. **Build relationships:** Successful traders build strong relationships with their suppliers and customers. This requires strong negotiation skills and the ability to communicate effectively and build trust. Be transparent with your suppliers and customers, and work to build long-term partnerships.

iv. **Price competitively:** Pricing is an important factor in the success of any trading business. To be successful, you need to price your products competitively. This requires an understanding of your costs and your competition. Monitor your prices regularly and adjust them as necessary to remain competitive.

v. **Market effectively:** Marketing is another key factor in the success of any trading business. Develop a marketing plan that includes social media, email marketing, and other tactics to reach your target audience. Use a mix of online and offline marketing to reach a wider audience.

vi. **Manage your inventory:** Managing inventory is critical for the success of any trading business. You need to have the right products in stock to meet demand, but you also need to avoid overstocking and tying up too much capital in inventory. Use inventory management software to help you track your inventory levels and make informed purchasing decisions.

vii. **Provide excellent customer service:** Customer service is essential for building a loyal customer base. Respond to customer inquiries promptly and provide helpful and friendly service. Offer easy returns and refunds, and be transparent about your policies.

viii. **Stay informed:** The trading industry is constantly evolving, so it is important to stay informed about the latest trends and developments. Attend industry events and read industry publications to keep up-to-date. Join online trading communities and forums to network with other traders and exchange ideas.

ix. **Stay focused:** Finally, staying focused on your goals and remaining committed to your vision is important. Trading can be challenging, and there will be ups and downs. But if you stay focused, work hard, and maintain a positive attitude, you can be successful.

Following these tips can increase your chances of success as a trader. Remember to stay focused, be creative, and be willing to adapt to changing market conditions.

3. Manufacturer

Manufacturers are entrepreneurs who create products from raw materials or components. This can include anything from clothing manufacturers to tech gadget makers. To be successful in manufacturing, entrepreneurs need to have a strong understanding of the production process and a deep knowledge of the products they create. Here are some tips to help you be a successful manufacturer:

i. **Understand the market:** The first step in becoming a successful manufacturer is understanding the market you are operating. Research the market, its trends, and its players. Understand what products are in demand and who your competitors are. This will help you identify opportunities and stay ahead of the curve.

ii. **Develop a strong product concept:** A strong product concept is the foundation of any successful manufacturing business. It should be unique, marketable, and fill market needs. Develop a prototype and test it with potential customers to get feedback before moving forward with production.

iii. **Create a solid business plan:** A solid business plan is essential for any manufacturing business. It should outline your vision, goals, and strategies for achieving them. It should also include financial projections, marketing strategies, and an analysis of your competitors.

iv. **Build a strong supply chain:** A strong supply chain is essential for the success of any manufacturing business. Identify reliable suppliers and partners who can provide the raw materials, components, and services you need to produce your products. Build long-term relationships with your suppliers to ensure a steady supply of high-quality materials.

v. **Invest in quality control:** Quality control is critical for any manufacturing business. Ensure that your products meet or exceed the quality standards of your industry. Implement quality control processes throughout production to ensure that each product is made to your specifications.

vi. **Manage your inventory:** Effective inventory management is critical for the success of any manufacturing business. You need to have the right materials and components in stock to meet demand, but you also need to avoid overstocking and tying up too much capital in inventory. Use inventory management software to help you track your inventory levels and make informed purchasing decisions.

vii. **Hire skilled employees:** Your employees are a key factor in the success of your manufacturing business. Hire skilled and experienced employees who are committed to quality and productivity. Invest in employee training and development to ensure that your employees are up-to-date with the latest production techniques and technologies.

viii. **Embrace technology:** Technology can help you streamline production processes, reduce costs, and improve quality. Use software and automation to improve inventory management, production planning, and quality control. Embrace new technologies and innovations to stay ahead of the curve.

ix. **Focus on sustainability:** Sustainable manufacturing is becoming increasingly important in today's world. Focus on reducing waste, conserving energy, and using eco-friendly materials and processes. This can help you reduce your environmental impact and appeal to consumers who are concerned about sustainability.

With hard work and determination, you can create high-quality products that meet your customers' needs and drive your business forward. By following these tips, you can increase your chances of success as a manufacturer. Remember to stay focused, be creative, and be willing to adapt to changing market conditions.

4. Network Marketing

Network marketing entrepreneurs sell products or services through a network of individuals who earn commissions based on the sales they generate. This can include multi-level marketing companies, direct sales organizations, and more. Network marketers must be skilled at building and maintaining relationships and convincing others to purchase the products or services they offer. To be successful in network marketing, here are some tips:

i. **Choose the right company:** Research a reputable company that offers high-quality products or services you believe in. Look for a company with a proven track record of success and a strong support system for its network marketers.

ii. **Build your network:** Network marketing relies on building and maintaining relationships with others. Start by reaching out to your personal network, including friends, family, and acquaintances. Attend networking events, use social media to connect with others, and be open to meeting new people.

iii. **Develop your sales skills:** Successful network marketers are great salespeople. Learn how to communicate the benefits of your products or services in a clear, concise, and compelling way. Develop your ability to handle objections and close sales.

iv. **Provide value:** Focus on providing value to your customers and network. This means understanding their needs and offering products or services to help them solve problems or meet demands. Be responsive to their questions and concerns, and follow up on promises.

v. **Stay organized:** Network marketing can be a busy and fast-paced business. Use technology to help you stay connected with your network and track your progress. Stay organized using tools such as a calendar, task list, and customer database.

vi. **Keep learning:** Network marketing is constantly evolving, so it's important to stay up-to-date on new trends and best practices. Attend training events, read industry blogs and books, and seek mentorship from successful network marketers.

vii. **Be persistent:** Success in network marketing takes time and effort. Be persistent and consistent in your actions, and don't get discouraged by rejection or setbacks. Stay focused on your goals and keep working towards them.

viii. **Build a personal brand:** As a network marketer, you are the face of your business. Build a personal brand that reflects your values and the benefits you offer to your customers. Use social media and other online platforms to showcase your expertise and build your reputation as a trustworthy and knowledgeable resource in your industry.

ix. **Provide excellent customer service:** In network marketing, your customers are the lifeblood of your business. Happy customers are more likely to recommend your products or services to others. Provide excellent customer service by responding to their needs promptly, following up on orders, and addressing any concerns they may have.

x. **Set realistic goals:** Setting achievable goals is an essential part of success in network marketing. Break down your goals into smaller, manageable steps, and track your progress along the way. Celebrate your successes, no matter how small, and learn from mistakes or setbacks.

xi. **Focus on duplication:** In network marketing, success is not just about your personal sales but also about the sales of your network. Focus on building a team of motivated and successful network marketers who can duplicate your efforts. Provide training and support to help them achieve their goals and encourage them to do the same for their own teams.

xii. **Be ethical:** The reputation of network marketing as a business model has been tarnished by unethical practices in some companies. Be transparent and honest in your dealings with others, and always operate with integrity. This will help you build a loyal customer base and attract like-minded individuals to your team.

xiii. **Embrace technology:** Technology can be a powerful tool for network marketers. Use social media, email marketing, and other digital tools to reach a wider audience and build your network. Stay up-to-date on new technologies and platforms to help you grow your business.

xiv. **Take care of yourself:** Building a successful network marketing business can be demanding and stressful. Take care of yourself by getting enough sleep, eating well, and exercising regularly. Make time for hobbies and activities you enjoy, and prioritize self-care to avoid burnout.

In summary, becoming a successful network marketer requires a combination of hard work, persistence, and strategic thinking. You can achieve your goals and build a thriving business by building your network, providing value to your customers, and staying up-to-date on best practices and new technologies.

5. Animal husbandry

Entrepreneurs in animal husbandry are those who raise animals for various purposes, such as for meat, dairy products, or breeding. This can include anything from small-scale backyard farming to large commercial operations. Successful animal husbandry entrepreneurs must have a deep knowledge of animal care and nutrition and strong business skills. To be successful in animal husbandry, here are some tips:

i. **Please choose the right animals:** Different animals have different needs and requirements, so it's important to choose the right animals for your operation. Consider factors such as the climate, the availability of feed and water, and the local market demand.

ii. **Invest in quality breeding stock:** The quality of your breeding stock will significantly impact the quality and productivity of your animals. Invest in high-quality animals with desirable traits, and take steps to maintain their health and genetic diversity.

iii. **Provide excellent animal care:** The welfare of your animals is critical to the success of your operation. Provide clean and comfortable living conditions, ensure access to fresh water and nutritious feed, and take steps to prevent and treat illnesses.

iv. **Develop a strong business plan:** Animal husbandry is a business, and it's important to approach it with a strong business plan. This should include market research, financial projections, and a marketing strategy.

v. **Seek out financing:** Starting and growing an animal husbandry operation can be capital-intensive. Seek financing options such as grants, loans, or partnerships to help fund your operation.

vi. **Build relationships with suppliers and buyers:** Building strong relationships with suppliers of feed, equipment, and other inputs, as well as buyers of your products, is crucial to the success of your operation. Find ways to add value to these relationships by offering high-quality products and reliable service.

vii. **Stay up-to-date on industry trends:** Animal husbandry is an evolving industry, and it's important to stay up-to-date on trends and best practices. Attend industry events, read industry publications, and seek opportunities for continuing education.

viii. **Be prepared for regulatory compliance:** Animal husbandry is subject to a wide range of local, state, and federal regulations. Be ready to comply with these regulations and seek professional advice if needed.

ix. **Leverage technology:** Technology can be a powerful tool for animal husbandry entrepreneurs. Use software and digital tools to manage your operation, track performance metrics, and communicate with suppliers and buyers.

x. **Network with other animal husbandry entrepreneurs:** Building relationships with other animal husbandry entrepreneurs can provide valuable support and advice. Look for opportunities to join industry associations, attend conferences, or participate in online forums.

In summary, becoming a successful animal husbandry entrepreneur requires a combination of strong animal care and business skills. You can build a successful and sustainable animal husbandry operation by providing excellent animal care, developing a strong business plan, and staying up-to-date on industry trends.

6. Farming

Farming entrepreneurs are those who cultivate crops or raise livestock for sale or for personal use. This can include everything from small-scale subsistence farming to large commercial operations. To be successful in farming, entrepreneurs must have a strong understanding of the local environment and the skills and knowledge necessary to cultivate healthy crops and livestock. They must also be able to manage their operation's financial and business aspects, such as marketing, sales, and distribution. To be successful in farming, here are some tips:

i. **Conduct market research:** Before starting a farm, it's important to conduct market research to understand the demand for different crops and livestock in your area. This will help you make informed decisions about what to grow and how to price and market your products.

ii. **Develop a strong business plan:** Farming is a business, and it's important to approach it with a strong business plan. This should include financial projections, marketing strategies, and a method for managing labour and other resources.

iii. **Please choose the right crops and livestock:** Different crops and livestock have different requirements, and choosing those well-suited to your local environment and market demand is important. Consider factors such as soil quality, climate, water availability, and pest and disease pressure.

iv. **Use sustainable farming practices:** Sustainable farming practices help preserve the environment and can be more cost-effective in the long run. Look for ways to conserve water, reduce pesticide and herbicide use, and promote soil health.

v. **Invest in high-quality equipment and inputs:** High-quality equipment and inputs can help you maximize your yield and minimize waste. Look for durable and reliable equipment, and use high-quality seeds, fertilizers, and other inputs.

vi. **Monitor and manage financial performance:** Farming can be a volatile business, and it's important to closely monitor your financial performance to identify areas for improvement. Track your expenses and revenues, and use this information to make informed decisions about your operation.

vii. **Build relationships with buyers:** Building strong relationships with buyers is critical to the success of your operation. Find ways to add value to these relationships by offering high-quality products and reliable service.

viii. **Stay up-to-date on industry trends:** The farming industry is constantly evolving, and it's important to stay up-to-date on trends and best practices. Attend industry events, read industry publications, and seek opportunities for continuing education.

ix. **Be prepared for regulatory compliance:** Farming is subject to a wide range of local, state, and federal regulations. Be prepared to comply with these regulations, and seek professional advice if needed.

x. **Network with other farming entrepreneurs:** Building relationships with other farming entrepreneurs can provide valuable support and advice. Look for opportunities to join industry associations, attend conferences, or participate in online forums.

In summary, becoming a successful farming entrepreneur requires a combination of strong agricultural and business skills. You can build a successful and sustainable farming operation by choosing the right crops and livestock, using sustainable farming practices, and closely monitoring your financial performance.

Reference List

Super, D. E. (1957). The psychology of careers: An introduction to vocational development. New York: Harper & Row Publishers.

Hill, N. (1998). The Law of Success, Volume 4. New York: Penguin Group.

Tracy, B. (2013). Time Management (The Brian Tracy Success Library). New York: AMACOM.

Clason, G. S. (2002). The Richest Man in Babylon. Signet.

Murphy, J. (2001). The Power of Your Subconscious Mind. Prentice Hall Press.

Kiyosaki, R. T. (2017). Rich Dad Poor Dad: What the Rich Teach Their Kids About Money That the Poor and Middle Class Do Not!. Plata Publishing.

Nemko, M. (2016). Career Courage: Discover Your Passion, Step Out of Your Comfort Zone, and Create the Success You Want. HarperOne.

Graham, B. (2003). The Intelligent Investor: The Definitive Book on Value Investing. HarperBusiness.

Hagstrom, R. G. (2013). The Warren Buffett Way. John Wiley & Sons.

Peale, N. V. (2003). The Power of Positive Thinking. Ballantine Books.

Schwartz, D. J. (2014). The Magic of Thinking Big. Simon & Schuster.

Cox, E., Bachkirova, T., & Clutterbuck, D. (Eds.). (2018). The Complete Handbook of Coaching (2nd ed.). SAGE Publications Ltd.

Brown, P. C., Roediger, H. L., & McDaniel, M. A. (2014). Make It Stick: The Science of Successful Learning. Harvard University Press.

Weyland, E. (2016). How to Study: 25th Anniversary Edition. Square One Publishers.

Duhigg, C. (2012). The Power of Habit: Why We Do What We Do in Life and Business. Random House.

Clear, J. (2018). Atomic Habits: An Easy & Proven Way to Build Good Habits & Break Bad Ones. Avery.

Zunker, V. G. (2019). Career Counseling: A Holistic Approach (9th ed.). Cengage Learning.

Lucas, S. E. (2014). The Art of Public Speaking (12th ed.). McGraw-Hill Education.

Briggs Myers, I., & Myers, P. B. (1995). Gifts Differing: Understanding Personality Type (Revised Edition). Davies-Black Publishing.

Jeff Keller, J. (2003). Attitude is Everything. Plume.

Canfield, J. (2005). The Success Principles: How to Get from Where You Are to Where You Want to Be. HarperCollins.

Byrne, R. (2013). The Business School. Wiley.

Clear, J. (2018). Atomic Habits: An Easy & Proven Way to Build Good Habits & Break Bad Ones. Avery.

About The Author

Lammuansang Tombing is a dynamic author, edupreneur, and psychologist and career development expert. With a Master's degree in Psychology and certified over 19 training course related to career development and counselling, Tombing has a deep understanding of the power of learning and skill in life. He is a passionate learner who has invested 7+ lakhs of rupees into enrolling in more than 45+ certification courses and is always seeking to expand his knowledge and expertise.

In addition to his academic and professional accomplishments, Tombing is also a published author, having written four books, including "Public Speaking Siam Diingdan," which has received critical acclaim. His dedication to his craft and passion for helping others achieve their full potential makes him the perfect guide for anyone looking to transform their life and career. His insights are invaluable for anyone seeking success and fulfilment in their personal and professional lives. Tombing is truly an exemplar of the power of learning and skill.

Bukim Growth's Resource

Bukim Growth is...?

Bukim Growth is the ultimate destination for personal and professional development. Our mission is to help you become a successful and fulfilled individual in all areas of your life.

Whether you are an employee looking to advance in your career, an employer seeking to build a strong and efficient team, an entrepreneur looking to grow your business, a student striving for academic excellence, or a parent seeking to raise happy and healthy children, Bukim Growth has something to offer you.

Our comprehensive training programs are designed to provide you with the skills and knowledge you need to succeed in your personal and professional endeavours. We offer a wide range of courses covering a variety of subjects, including entrepreneurship, leadership, personal growth, sales, parenting, relationship, and more.

In addition to our training programs, we also offer services such as counselling, consultancy, and coaching to help you navigate the challenges of life and achieve your goals. Our team of experts is here to support and guide you on your journey to success.

Choose Bukim Growth and take the first step towards a better and more fulfilling life.

Sign up today at www.bukimgrowth.com

Dear reader,

Have you ever wished to enhance your personal and professional life to seven times better than where you currently are? If so, Bukim Growth is here to help!

We are excited to introduce you to our one-year course that is designed to take you on an incredible journey of self-discovery and transformation. Our platform is the first and only one of its kind that offers a comprehensive online course to help you learn most of the important skills to be successful in life and career.

Our course is a combination of live and recorded lectures that are self-paced and certification-based. We offer a range of skills that will benefit you in various aspects of your life, such as public speaking, leadership, sales, entrepreneurship, parenting, relationship building, job hunting, book writing, study skills, and counselling.

We understand that life can be hectic, and you may have limited time to learn new skills. That is why we have designed our course to be flexible, so you can learn whenever you want, wherever you like, and on your own comfort zone. Our live classes are conducted once per week to ensure that any doubts you may have are cleared.

If you are unable to complete the course in one year, you can attempt the exam the following year. We do not focus on overwhelming you with data dumps. Instead, we teach you the most relevant things and practical ideas to help you succeed.

Investing in yourself is the best decision you can make. Our one-year course is designed to help you grow personally and professionally, and it is an opportunity you do not want to miss. Our website: www.bukimgrowth.com | +91 8794970270

Sign up today and join our community of successful learners!

Best regards,
Lammuansang Tombing
Founder & CEO
Bukim Growth

For academic institutions:

Dear Sir/Madam,

I am pleased to offer your school and students our **Multiple Intelligence Psychometric Aptitude Test (MIPAT) and Study Skill Training program.**

At the career group counselling session, our team will carry out MIPAT, which is a Psychometric Test that identifies each student's multiple intelligences (**linguistic, logical-mathematical, visual-spatial, musical, bodily-kinaesthetic, Naturalistic, interpersonal, and intrapersonal**). In addition, our team of career guidance experts will help them understand their skills and interests while introducing them to different career options available in today's market that suit them.

The Study Skill Training component of the program is **used widely in developed countries, and we invest over 8 Lakhs rupees** for research and to get certified by 39 different institutions, including Sikkim University, Rajasthan University, Counsel India, Bodhami, HealthyMinds World, Graphy (Unacademy), Mindpriests, and IAP Career College (USA) to name a few. **We are trustedpartners** with some of these institutions and **are the only provider of this type of training in the entire northeast region.**

We provide solutions for students who are unsure of what course to take or what career to pursue after high school, and higher secondary. We have conducted **over 200 Career Guidance Seminars** in many schools, and colleges, and have received overwhelmingly positive feedback from students and faculty members. Our techniques have proved to help students reduce the time it takes to **memorize their notes by 50%.** The training will include tools such as the **Wheel of Life, Mind Mapping, Speed Reading, Mnemonic techniques, Goal setting, and Neuro-linguistic programming (NLP).**

We will **provide you with all of your student reports (PDF) for your future use and train your teachers for free** on how to effectively read and utilize those reports in order to promote the success of your institution.

Since we are aware of the importance of our training for students and the potential impact it has on their future, **we offer our services at a reasonable price.**

We are confident that this program, featuring certified trainers and proven study skills techniques, will be an invaluable resource for your students and will help them succeed in their academic and personal endeavours. We have attached a detailed proposal for your review, including information about **our packages/pricing, credential, program offerings, topic details, extra information and questionnaire for MI Psychometric test.**

Thank you for considering this proposal, and please do not hesitate to contact us if you have any query | Call +91 8794970270 | bukimgrowth@gmail.com | Website; www.bukimgrowth.com

.

Sincerely,
Lammuansang Tombing
Founder & CEO
Bukim Growth

Subject: **Request to conduct Midbrain activation for the benefit of your school's students.**

Dear Sir,

We would like to request your consideration for conducting Midbrain activation for the students at **[School Name]**. Midbrain activation is a unique learning technique that allows children to influence their performance by stimulating the part of the brain associated with memory and learning. Midbrain activation uses specially designed exercises to stimulate three key areas: Maths, Memory and Development (MMD). It helps a child to develop their abilities, by unlocking the power of their mind, through a combination of cognitive and physical exercises.

Midbrain activation boosts concentration, concentration span, speed of recall, memorizing skills and creative visualization abilities. It is considered to be a safe and natural way to increase the potential of a child to the fullest. The midbrain activation program also helps the child realign their focus and encourages them to use the power of their imagination. Some of the benefits are:

1. **Improved sensory abilities**: One of the primary benefits of midbrain activation is its ability to enhance the five senses of the human body. This is achieved by stimulating the area of the brain responsible for sensory processing, leading to sharper senses and increased sensory awareness.

2. **Balanced brain hemispheres:** Another benefit of midbrain activation is its ability to balance the left and right hemispheres of the brain. By balancing these two halves, individuals are better able to utilize both their analytical and creative faculties, leading to more well-rounded and effective thinking.

3. **Increased brain connectivity:** Midbrain activation can also help to improve the speed and efficiency with which information is transferred between the two hemispheres of the brain. This leads to faster processing and increased overall brain connectivity.

4. **Improved long-term memory:** A further benefit of midbrain activation is its ability to improve long-term memory. By stimulating the midbrain, individuals are better able to process and retain information, leading to improved memory and recall.

5. **Increased learning speed:** Finally, midbrain activation has been shown to increase learning speed, allowing individuals to learn and absorb new information at a faster pace. This can be particularly beneficial for students or those in professional fields that require ongoing learning and development. Overall, midbrain activation has many potential benefits that are worth considering for those looking to improve their cognitive abilities and overall well-being.

We believe that such a program would allow your students to reach their full potential and excel in their studies. We also believe that this is the kind of learning strategy that will have an impact for many years to come.

We would be grateful for your consideration of this request and look forward to your response.

Thank you for your time and consideration.

Sincerely,
Lammuansang Tombing
Founder & CEO
Bukim Growth

Subject: **Request to conduct a relationship seminar for the benefit of your members.**

Dear Sir/Madam,

We are writing on behalf of Bukim Growth, an organization dedicated to providing workshops, seminars, and counseling to promote healthy relationships. We are passionate about helping people form and maintain healthy relationships, both with themselves and with those in their lives, and we believe that providing our services to the community as a whole can be very beneficial.

We are excited to offer our services to you and your org. members. We offer a two-sessions Relationship Seminar that can help your members improve the interpersonal relationships in their lives. The seminar includes topics such as the importance of communication, healthy boundaries, understanding conflict and dispute resolution, the essence of love, and much more. We would be happy to customize the seminar to meet any specific needs that your members might have.

The seminar is presented in an interactive, encouraging, and non-judgmental way, and we strive to provide each participant with the tools and resources they need to create and maintain meaningful relationships. We believe our Relationship Seminar can be a great addition to your church programming, and we would love to discuss the possibility of bringing our program to your church and its members. Please feel free to contact me directly anytime at 8794970270 or by email at bukimgrowth@gmail.com

We look forward to hearing from you.

.

Sincerely,
Lammuansang Tombing
Founder & CEO
Bukim Growth

Subject: **Request to conduct DMIT lifetime test for the benefits of your school' students.**

Dear Sir/Madam,

We are excited to introduce you to the benefits of conducting a lifetime DMIT Test for your students. DMIT stands for Dermatoglyphics Multiple Intelligence Test, a specially designed test designed to help each individual recognize their own uniqueness and capabilities.

This test is administered at the onset of the individual's school career and evaluates potential learning styles, personal passions, multiple intelligences, and other pertinent personality factors. It is intended to build a lifelong profile of each student and identify unique capabilities, interests, and core skills that are best suited for that individual.

The benefits of the DMIT Test for your student population include accurate identification of learning styles and strengths that can serve as a basis for career counseling and better academic decision-making, greater introspection and self-reflection, and more personalized feedback for each student.

We understand that each school has unique needs and goals, and we look forward to working with you to implement a customized DMIT test program that will best benefit your student population.

Thank you for this opportunity and we look forward to hearing from you.

.

Sincerely,
Lammuansang Tombing
Founder & CEO
Bukim Growth

Subject: Training Program Proposal: Basic Counseling Skills, Public Speaking Skills, and Child Psychology/Care for Teachers.

Dear,

I am writing to propose a training program for our teachers that will focus on developing basic counselling skills, public speaking skills, and knowledge of child psychology and care. As you are aware, our school is committed to providing our students with the best possible education, and we believe that this training program will help us achieve that goal.

The purpose of the training program is to equip our teachers with the necessary skills and knowledge to effectively communicate with and care for our students. The program will cover topics such as active listening, empathy, effective communication, public speaking, child psychology, and care, among others.

We intend to hold the training program over a period of four weeks, with each week focusing on a specific topic. The program will be conducted by qualified and experienced trainers who have a wealth of experience in counselling, public speaking, and child psychology.

We believe that this training program will have a positive impact on our teachers and students alike. By developing basic counselling skills, our teachers will be better equipped to deal with any emotional or psychological issues that our students may face. Additionally, by improving their public speaking skills, our teachers will be able to deliver engaging and informative lessons that will capture the attention of our students.

The cost of the training program will be [insert cost here], and we believe that it is a worthwhile investment in the future of our school. We are confident that this training program will have a positive impact on our teachers and our students and we hope that you will consider our proposal.

Thank you for your consideration, and we look forward to hearing from you soon.

.

Sincerely,
Lammuansang Tombing
Founder & CEO
Bukim Growth

Subject: **Request to conduct a leadership training program for the benefit of your Youth Members.**

Dear Sir/Madam,

I am writing to request permission to conduct a leadership training program at our school. I believe that this program would be a valuable and beneficial event for our students, and I hope that you will consider granting me permission to organize and host it.

The leadership training program will focus on helping individuals to develop the skills and knowledge needed to be effective leaders in their school, community, and future careers. It will cover a wide range of topics, including communication, teamwork, and problem-solving.

The program will be led by experienced leaders from the local community who will provide valuable insights and practical advice on how to be an effective leader. It will also include interactive activities and discussions to help students apply what they learn to their own leadership experiences.

I am confident that this program will be well received by our youth and will provide them with valuable skills and knowledge that they can use to become successful leaders in the future.

Thank you for considering my request. I look forward to discussing this further with you and obtaining your approval to conduct the leadership training program.

.

Sincerely,
Lammuansang Tombing
Founder & CEO
Bukim Growth

Dear Sir/Madam,

I hope this letter finds you well. I am writing to propose a **'Mental Health and Teenage Issues'** Seminar to help the **junior, intermediate/junior high, and senior students** of your Sunday school. As a career counsellor and biblical counsellor, I understand the need of our teenage today. This seminar is highly valued, as it was successful in the previous program that I conducted at another church.

The seminar will focus on helping teenagers deal with current stress, depression, anxiety, and relationship problems. It will be divided into two sessions: **the first session will cover Mental Health, including the wheel of life, cognitive restructuring, the right attitude, reading the Bible, and Christian life.** The second session will **cover Happiness, Relationship Issues, Porn Addiction, Game Addiction, Drug Addiction, and Study Problems**. Our teaching will be based on the Bible, but we will not focus on doctrine or sensitive issues that may be different for different churches.

This program will be **two sessions, each 1.5 hours long,** and we can conduct it in your normal Sunday school program on two separate days or plan it for one single day as a special seminar. I am confident that this seminar will help your teenage members to cope with their mental and emotional struggles, and to live a healthy and fulfilling life.

I believe this seminar will be a valuable asset to your church community, and I would be honoured to lead this program for the youth of your church. **We have attached a detailed proposal for your review, including information about our accreditation, the program offerings, topic details, and extra information.**

Thank you for considering this proposal, and please do not hesitate to contact us if you have any queries | Call- +91 8794970270 | bukimgrowth@gmail.com | Website; www.bukimgrowth.com

.

Sincerely,
Lammuansang Tombing
Founder & CEO
Bukim Growth

www.ingramcontent.com/pod-product-compliance
Lightning Source LLC
Chambersburg PA
CBHW031128130726
47988CB00006B/2276